No Id

CW01558385

two months on the road with Leonard Cohen

A real-life account of the daily
fiction surrounding backstage life

the second edition:
leaner, picturesquer, betterer

by Leif Bodnarchuk

ISBN 978-1-291-89253-6

Find Leif on the internetz:
leifb73.com

all photos by author
except back cover shot of author,
taken by Dan Weingartner

For Davy, Sean, Steve, and Arlene

August 6, 2012; 5.45 a.m.

My alarm sounds and my eyes pop open.
I mumble; 'Leonard Cohen. Better get going.'
My wife Elaine rolls over. 'Bring back milk.' She nods off.
I look to the bedroom door and a sliver of light sneaks in.
It'll be 63 days until I sleep in this bed again.

Hello.
I'm Leif.
I'm a roadie.
I maintain electric guitars and amplifiers. I'm not a real author, I'm just a guy who likes to write. This is the second edition of *No Ideas*.

WHAT HAPPENS IN THIS BOOK?

It's a diary. I go places and do things. It isn't about Leonard Cohen, and it's not aimed at his fans. He appears only occasionally.

A few words of caution: like the previous edition, this book contains 'bad' language. Should the occasional flowering of *effs, esses, bees, pees and cees* drive you to complain, this is probably not for you.

This book is primarily about one roadie and his roadie world: real, imaginary, and sometimes overlapping.

Between Heaven and Hell there's the life you live.

How and whatever you find this book to be, I hope you like it.

GET OUT OF BED

I'm doing my best not to fall down the stairs.
Munching on some dusty cereal I think to the future.
What will the world look like in 63 days?
Will it be at peace? Will bee numbers rise?
Will I have grown a golden mane, flowing in the breeze as I tap-dance home on a candy rainbow?
No one knows.
I'm only certain of one thing: I have to get out and live for 63 days.
I have to leave the house and join the 2012 Leonard Cohen *Old Ideas* tour.

1

PERSONNEL

BAND

Leonard Cohen, *Vocals & Guitar*
Roscoe Beck, *MD / Basses / Backing Vocals*
Neil Larsen, *Keyboards / Accordian*
Rafael Gayol, *Drums / Percussion*
Mitch Watkins, *Guitar / Backing Vocals*
Javier Mas, *Guitar / Laud / Archilaud / Banduria*
Alexandru Bublitchi, *Violin*
Sharon Robinson, *Vocals*
Charley Webb, *Vocals / Clarinet / Guitar*
Hattie Webb, *Vocals / Harp*

CREW

Mike *Tour Manager*
Dave *Production Manager*
Joseph *Road Manager*
Ed *Producer*
Wade *Tour Accountant*
Renee *Production Assistant*
Kezban *Personnel Coordinator*
Paul *Stage Manager*
Ryan *Lighting Director*
Mark *FOH Sound Engineer*
Jon *Sound Engineer*
Russ *Monitor Engineer*
PANTS — *Sound Engineer*
Maz *Back Stage Co-ordinator*
Nicky *Wardrobe Supervisor*
Dan *Drums & Keys Technician*
Mickey *Guitar Technician*
Chris *Bass, Guitar & Harp Technician*
Leif Bodnarchuk, *Guitar Technician & Boffin*
Benni *Backline Technician*
John *Tour Rigger*
Lorca *Product Manager / Photographer*
Tom *Merchandise*

2

August 2012

"It's a curious thing, Frodo, setting out from home. You get out that door and you have no idea if you're going to be hit by a bus, a train, an airplane, or by an irate taxi driver named Hammer who insists upon you repeatedly asking him the time."

-Bambot Baggins
  (the one you never heard from)

August 6: Away to Gent

My taxi driver's name wasn't Hammer. After saying goodbye to Elaine and the kids, *Not-Hammer* drove me to George Best Belfast City Airport, where I boarded a flying machine to Birmingham.

I arrived in Birmingham hours before the Brussels flight was due to leave. After some pointless retail therapy I bumped into our stage manager, Paul. We caught up quickly while waiting for the check-in desk to open. I think the airline was called *We Fly to Brussels Or We'll Die Trying*.

When we landed in Belgium I met a couple of new faces, John the rigger and Nicky the wardrobe mistress. It turns out Nicky was just on my flight. I find this business of travelling to work a little weird; you can share space with a colleague and be unaware. When you're introduced to them, and realise you were staring right at them in an airport, you start searching your memory for anything stupid you might have said or done in their presence.

Fortunately I wasn't a knob. I think.

I've been such a tool on so many occasions in this business. Since my twenties a steady diet of alcohol and occasional drugs has been at the centre of some very silly and sometimes cringeworthy behaviour. At this stage of my life and career, I prefer to make a healthy first impression *before* I become an obnoxious twit.

We were supposed to meet with a few others and travel to Gent together, but they've been delayed.

The four of us present hopped into a waiting van. On the way I was mindful of my behaviour in the company of new colleagues. Maybe they'll think I'm normal.

The beautiful city of Gent was an hour's drive away.

Hotel.

A stone's throw from the reception desk is the bar. It's bright, airy, and you can't miss anyone sitting in it.

Familiar faces.

Amid a cast sat the boss, Leonard.

After a handshake, a brief *how are you* and *I can't complain,* I threw my luggage into my room and returned to enjoy a beer.

After some beers came a trip out for some noodles, and around midnight those whose flights were delayed finally arrived at the hotel.

I went *home* to my room. As a general rule I don't unpack my things; I prefer to live out of a suitcase. People who fill hotel wardrobes and drawers are weird. It's just going to take them longer to pack up when it's time to leave.

But I have to get my underpants out. It's a baseline convenience. I'm not a total vagabond. Pulling out a change of clothing for the morning makes you feel like you're home.

August 7: Gent, Rehearsals

You need to know about *backline*. In the touring world backline is the collection of gear musicians and technicians use. It's basically musical instruments and tools. We have five backline technicians, or *techs*. We don't bother ourselves with lights and P.A. speakers, just as lighting and sound techs don't concern themselves with guitar strings and drum sticks.

Around 10 a.m., I awaited transport outside the hotel. I met Benni the drum tech. He's German and a fan of Earl Grey tea and Coca Cola.

Dan is in charge of all things keyboard. Originally from Boston he now lives in England. Wearing sunglasses, he emerged from the hotel like a camp Terminator.

The morning grew warmer and last to arrive were Chris and Mickey. Chris is a real live Texan who wears cowboy boots and smokes American Spirit cigarettes. He looks after the bass equipment, and the Webb Sisters' acoustic guitars and harps.

Mickey is a Londoner. With a slew of clients under his belt like Simple Minds, The Offspring, and Elvis Costello, Mickey looks after Leonard and Javier's acoustic and nylon-stringed guitars.

Met by a man with a van, we set off to the rehearsal venue.

Flanders Expo is a big dark box of a room, a wide open space where cherry-pickers (mobile elevated platforms) lift riggers to install hanging points. Trucks with 45-foot trailers park side by side, awaiting the appropriate time to unload. The place is more like an airplane hangar.

Things are always slow on a first day. We knew it would be a while until the backline was needed on stage. There's no stage really, we're setting everything up on the concrete floor. But we're assembling it all as if it was a real performance, so for the sake of argument we'll call the performance area a stage.

OH GOD THE RUGS

The only aesthetic change from the last tour is new rugs. We used to lay pretty Persian-style rugs on stage, but since we're scheduled to play outdoor shows, it was felt the Persians were best spared. We had time to kill before unloading the backline so we unrolled the new rugs and had a go.

They're shit.

It took some creativity, and management, by those whose pay-grades accord with artistic decisions, to cobble together a look that wasn't... horrid. These new rugs are sun-bleached and almost parallelogram in shape.

Arranged as they were (complete with trip hazards) they belonged not on stage but in a student flat. But... Team Backline aren't paid to make creative decisions, we're servants to the Creative Wish. We're the ugly fairy godmothers in black. We breathe life into your fantasy.

I shan't bore you with the minutiae of waiting for lights to rise, unloading the truck, positioning the backline, risers (platform things you see drummers on), drums, B3 organ, keyboards, bass rig, guitar amps, microphones etc. Once it was all in place I was finally able to spread out, plug things in, and see what I was really working with.

IF TECHNICAL GEEKERY BORES YOU, LOOK AWAY NOW

On this tour I'll be looking after guitarist Mitch Watkins. I'll handle his guitars, amps and pedals, and try my best to make him feel at ease on stage. I'll be doing similar for Javier, but limited to his electric guitars and amp.

I haven't met Mitch in person. Today I'll acquaint myself with his gear. His amp is a Fender Supersonic. His pedal-board sports an Ibanez TS10 Tube Screamer Classic distortion pedal, an MXR Dyna Comp, a Boss GT-3 guitar effects processor, and a Moog Low Pass Filter. The audio chain is linear except in the Moog's case, plugged into the GT3's effects loop.

Guitars: trade secret. That, and I can't be bothered to list them. They're just guitars. Between Mitch and Javier I have ten on my roster. Thankfully they're mostly electric.

Javier plays electric guitar on a handful of songs. He uses a Fender Telecaster and prehistoric Gibson SG. His amp is a Fender '65 Princeton reissue and they don't make 'em like they used to. During transit a footswitch socket retreated into the amp.

After opening the amp I bled its filter capacitors, making the innards safe to probe with bare fingers. Locating the socket (and thankfully the nut), a dash of nail polish on the screw threads ensured it won't shake loose again.

Nail polish?

Every self-respecting roadie keeps nail polish handy. You should also be able to sew.

Anyway, that sunken socket was the only pressing maintenance issue.

TECHNICAL GEEKERY IS OVER NOW

After ensuring everything was operational it was time to call it a day and head to the hotel for a beer. I finally met Mitch. He doesn't drink but that doesn't stop me. We talked for a while and I made sure to behave.

When I got to my room I noticed my legs were sore. You wouldn't know it from this diary but the day was busy enough.

Life is hard

August 8: Gent, Rehearsals

My legs are tired and sore. I'm either totally out of shape, or the Expo's concrete floor is taking its toll. Somewhere there's a tiny violin playing a sarcastic song for me.

I had breakfast with Raf.

He was eating scrambled eggs. 'So Leif, what have you been doing with yourself?'

'I inherited my great-uncle's estate.'

'Oh I'm sorry for your loss.'

8

'Yeah his stuffed hand is the new TV remote holder.'

At 10 a.m. a man with a van drove Team Backline to the Expo.
We're expecting the band later today.
I still haven't had an in-depth technical discussion with either Mitch or Javier, and this makes me a little edgy. In this job you strive to know what your artist wants before they want it. When they arrive I'll have to corner each of them.
Everyone's different, I don't know how Mitch likes his guitar handed to him, which is the fail-safe, what piece of gear is the most precious, how he moves, what he expects me to do for him, or when he'll think me too eager. Sometimes a musician wants the tech to back off and let them breathe.
It normally takes a few shows for tech and musician to experience the mind-meld. Here in the beginning it's vital to be friendly and open to anything.

ROADIE TALK

Over the years I've learnt patience is better than trying to get ahead of the game. I don't want to tinker unnecessarily with Mitch's guitars (other than brief checks to confirm they're neither broken nor on fire). I think it's best to ensure the gear is in adequate working order, and leave it at that.
When considering aesthetics, how and where cables are laid, where amplifiers sit, etc., it's better to start off ugly and simple. Here's what you don't want to happen:
'Hi Mitch, I've made some cable-looms and modified your amp so it powers the pedals when you switch it on.'
'Dude, that's not how it goes together.'
'But...'

At lunch I accidentally bit a chunk of my tongue off.

Everyone knows what a soundcheck is. Roadies do *line-check*. Roadies (including sound engineers who hate being called roadies) turn everything on, check the microphones and instruments, and ensure we're ready for action.
After line-check Leonard arrived to listen to the P.A. system and do a soundcheck on his own. An hour later the band arrived.

At last, Mitch and I get down to business; we discussed which guitars he would use for which songs, alternate tunings, capo positions, and other fine details unworthy of print.

Leonard and the band soundchecked and everything was great, but suddenly the P.A. started acting strangely. Intermittent clicks and pops. Intermittent issues are the worst; when you can't recreate the problem and identify its nature, you have a frustrating puzzle.

They carried on through the glitches. Mitch and I started to get used to each other and everything fared smoothly for us at least.

I hate the rugs. Aside from their ugliness, they're a patchwork of trip hazards. But Leonard likes them so we'll have to make them work.

We finished at 9.30 p.m.

I put the guitars back in their cases, covered up the amps (the Expo's roof was a bit leaky) and had a beer in a makeshift green room.

Fact attack: a *green room* is basically a common area for band and crew to relax in, a cove of drinks and snacks.

Apparently in Shakespeare's day the green room was a patch of garden, stage left. In France, you don't call stage left *scène à gauche*, you simply call it *jardin*. Anyway…

Maz is in charge of green room things. Not only does she make the place look nice but she liaises with caterers to communicate the various dietary requirements of our bunch. For this tour I eat vegan.

I picked up a sandwich and left the Expo.

The sky was the deepest shade of blue, the sun locked down.

The audio guys spent extracurricular hours trying to sort out the nightmare bug.

August 9: Gent, Rehearsals

I woke up and thought *What have I done?* Keeping a diary is a pain in the ass. Aiming for a daily dose of presentable prose began to feel like a job on top of a job.

I stared at myself in the mirror. Long and hard.

'They're going to find out.'

'No, I swear, I'll be good.'

'You always say that. Do you remember *Henri le couteau?*'

'You said you'd never bring that up again.'

I smiled thinly. 'Relax. It's our little secret.'

I shared another breakfast with Raf. He used to photograph red-carpet dos in Hollywood. It always strikes me as fascinating, how people with talent are just plain... talented. After he upped and left me talentlessly staring into my bread, a couple of the sound guys sat down. I got nosey and asked about the issues they faced yesterday.

You've probably seen a mixing desk. Look for someone who thinks their ponytail is descended from God's own beard, and chances are they're operating a mixing desk. It's that big thing with a zillion knobs and faders — some people call them *sliders*. That word hurts my ears. Anyway these godly-maned sound engineers use mixing desks to sculpt the soundscape of a concert. And the desk you see in among the audience is but one of two.

What you hear in the audience bears little resemblance to the sound on stage. There's another mixing desk in the wings, operated by second demigod who provides a whole different mix for the musicians.

So like most bands we have a front-of-house (FOH) desk and a monitor desk.

TECHNICAL TALK

Both our desks are digital. Digital problems are different from analogue. Time is literally of the essence with digital equipment. All those ones and zeros need to flow coherently, and this stream is controlled by digital clocks. If the various clocks aren't perfectly synchronised, audible snips and blips tell the engineer something isn't right. It's an unfortunate symptom — one would hope such errors might be announced in visual cues, but that's not how it goes.

Problem bottom line, in layman's terms: *clocks*.

END TECH TALK

My legs are getting back in shape. Pity I can't say the same for Maz. Her knee is kaput; in a couple days she'll be hobbling about on a clumsy support brace.

After seeing the band play last night and talking with Mitch and Javier, I felt confident to get ahead today. I got my soldering iron out and made some cables, sheathing them in *snakeskin*, replacing some spaghetti-style cabling. Now Mitch's setup looks a bit more sleek. I made a pedal-board for Javier: tuner, reverb/vibe foot-switch, power supply and chorus pedal.

God that sounds dull.

'Hey what did you do today?'
'I melted an alloy with a hot pencil and guitars worked.'
'Hey good for you I'm gonna go talk to that other guy.'
They're going to find out.

Today's rehearsal was good for me and Mitch. He's getting used to having me as a tech and I'm growing accustomed to his style. We aim to be a two-man hurricane of awesomeness.

The day wasn't so fruitful for the sound department. Again they stayed late to fathom their audio woes. Team Backline was of no use so we returned to the hotel.

I had a few beers and went to bed.

August 10: Gent, Rehearsals

Today is the final rehearsal day.

Every day this week I've emerged from the hotel in morning shade and clambered into a van with tinted glass. The van drives into the venue and I find myself in a windowless expanse. It's summer out there but the majority of light I see is human-made. Occasionally an angel's sunray leaks from a distant open door.

When we finish the evenings are dusky or dark. I've seen little of the sun in four days and it was only for my love of tea that this disconnect became apparent.

Among my tools I carry a kettle. I wanted to clean it.

I boiled a little water. I had to tip it outdoors.

The fucking sun nearly ripped my eyes out when I went outside. I looked like a vampire — not the immortal, six-pack chested, girl-magnet teenage vamp. No I was a wincing, hobbling, and slightly overweight mess of a man, scurrying back inside like a terrified mouse to a comfortable gloom.

On any final rehearsal day it's wise to have a relaxed atmosphere. You want the musicians to enter a calm, easy-going environment, not a hospital triage. My usual rehearsal routine, for any band, is to go like the clappers for the first few days, and take it easy on the last.

Effortless tasks. Polish. Tidying. *Idiot-proofing.*

If I should get sick, anyone stepping into my shoes will need some visual cues to help them. Labels, some arrows made of coloured tape, and some chinagraph (grease) pencil markings all help.

Today is a dress rehearsal; the boys and girls in the band looked sharp in their stage garb. Undeterred by the continuing saga of audio pops and clicks, Leonard and the band played a three hour set.

The audio guys are going greyer by the minute dealing with the digital hitches.

Mitch and I are finding our groove. Like the clocks it's essential to sync, ensuring smooth transitions. Otherwise it's a faff; people pay good money for tickets and they don't want to see a clumsy ballet. Dead air on stage is the enemy.

After rehearsal it was time for *load-out*, my favourite part of the day. It's time to move on. The dead-air rule applies to load-outs too. The lighting department are itching to get their gear down and packed up, and our stuff is in the way. The toys need to go into the boxes and the boxes need to go in the truck.

We've been here for days. Packing the truck and seeing its doors close gives a sense of achievement: *We've done something and we're going somewhere else.*

Now the challenge is thirst. With the backline in the truck it was time for a beer; I pounded two bottles of Jupiler on the way to the hotel.

I opened my room door; the light was on.

This is strange I thought.

I always ensure the lights are off before I leave. I thought some more; *fuck it.* I chocked the door with my foot and threw in my bag and steel-toe shoes — one at a time, like a cricket bowler.

'Aieee!' came a pained voice from within.

The poor housekeeping guy.

He had just finished turning down the bed, and in the line of fire he took a steely boot to the dome. The Belgian went down like a bag of hammers.

'I don't have time for this shit,' I muttered.

I dragged his limp body to the threshold, his polyester jacket sparking against the dry carpet. I wedged the door ajar with his outstretched hand.

His colleagues should be able to identify him by his rings.

Into his flaccid hand I crumpled a ten euro note.

I went to the bar.

August 11: Gent, Technical Rehearsal

I'm hungover. Bastard. I'm not pleased with myself, but it's not really my fault. Dave made me drink. Him and Dupuis. More on Dupuis later.

In this business a hangover is almost never a crime, but some folks (i.e. me) don't do well under the spell. You'd think I would've learned by now.

FLASHBACK

May 2008: Leonard is rehearsing for the Fredericton dates, his first tour in 15 years. We had finished rehearsals in the venue. We were all set up and ready to go. The night before the very first show, the demon, Dupuis, paid me a memorable visit. He is never announced. He comes when you don't want him; with an invisible hand he clutches your shoulder and whispers in your ear: *drink you fool, drink!*

Fortunately I waded through the mental mire and opening night was a success. But I vowed to prevent Dupuis from darkening my mind on a 'school night'.

Do I listen to my vows? Shit no.

BACK TO THE PRESENT (OR FUTURE, WHATEVER)

Today I am a shell of a man who barely knows what he's doing. Last night Dupuis bundled me into a wheelbarrow and tipped me over a metaphysical cliff face. At the bottom I crash-landed onto a bed of dented cars and bin liners filled with soiled jeans.

I don't know how, but I peeled myself out of bed and met a man with a van. Dan was my saviour. He had pills. They faded Dupuis' shadow and for a time I forgot the demon's face.

Daylight. Today we're setting up outdoors in Sint-Pietersplein for opening night; the gods may have cursed me with a sore head, but they've mercifully stretched time in my favour: the show is tomorrow. Today we set up in situ, another chance to get it right.

You might think it odd that after five days at Flanders Expo we're setting up for yet another rehearsal. I'm not privy to these executive decisions, but I can say I like the measured pace. Today's goal is to set everything up as if we were doing a gig — but not do a gig.

Backstage is a network of dressing rooms, production offices, kitchens, wardrobe stores and torture chambers. All these things are accommodated by Saint Peter's Abbey Cultural Centre, a welcome relief from the day's heat. We're transported back in time by cloisters and catacombs, sagging lead-lined windows, and a serene quadrangle. The quad is a place of meditative quiet and the stone floor has been infiltrated by grass. In the centre of the court stands a well.

No, I didn't spit into it

The lights levitated; time for Team Backline to amble into gear.

ROADIE GIBBERISH

First Team Backline lays black carpets, used to deaden the sound and make things look nice. In 44-foot runs they're ribbed like corduroy trousers. We're supposed to centre and tape them down but... my gaffer tape, measuring tape and chalk are all inside my workbox — buried in the truck.

God damnit.

My tools are still buried because dock space is limited. I had to go on the scrounge, but the blacks finally went down.

After all my complaining about those shitty rugs in rehearsals, we're not using them. Instead we're laying the old ones, the reds, because we're afraid of inclement weather ruining those 'new', precious and derelict pieces of crap. I'm glad; laying the reds is easy.

15

After the rugs come the risers. To assemble them you insert aluminium legs into sockets and secure the terribly complicated process with a wing-bolt. Even a guy with one arm and a hangover can do that. The risers should be placed according to a predetermined layout but... these carpets don't have the current layout spiked. *God damnit again.*

Spiking: denoting an item's physical placement with tape or marker. You spike risers, microphone stands, monitors etc., so you always know where they go. At Expo we spiked the crappy rugs, not the reds.

It took us a while to agree on placement and this process would have been quicker with a copy of a stage-plot. But no one had one.

I made one:

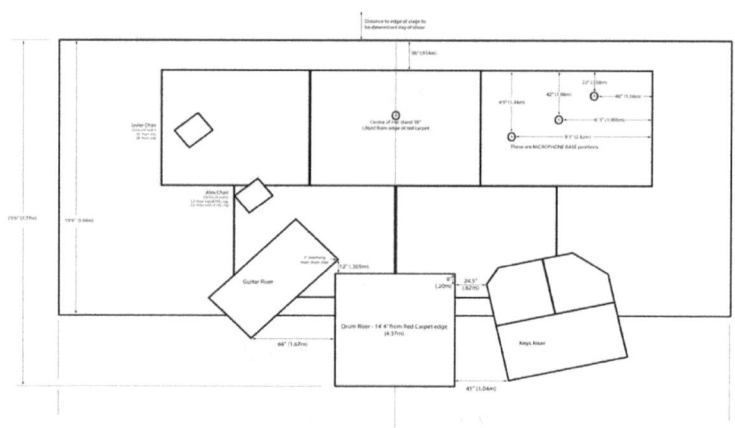

END ROADIE GIBBERISH

We set up the backline and had lunch while the audio guys placed microphones. We have the same catering team that looked after us in the Expo and the food was great.

Later, Leonard came by for a soundcheck on his own. He sings, and plays his black Godin guitar. When he saw the red rugs he said he loved them. He asked what was wrong with them in the first place.

I muttered something and walked away backwards, smiling too much.

After troubleshooting and employing backups for backups, the audio team ironed out their own wrinkles. There were no pops, glitches, nor any muttered curses from the engineers. It came together.

We got away from the site around 8 p.m.

Must resist beer.

August 12: Opening Night

After a lone breakfast I spent some time writing and at 11.30 a.m. got into a van and went to the gig.

Most of the equipment was already set up so I spent a half-hour ensuring my work area was ship-shape. I changed some guitar strings, ate lunch, and made mental notes of this difficult life.

At lunch news of a potential problem began to spread. Roscoe had somehow taken a quick and severe illness. *Can he do the show?*

Scenarios and contingencies followed but the facts were still coming in. Rumour says Leonard visited an ailing Roscoe in his hotel room, flashed the trademark grin and assessed the situation.

The show must go on. Yawn. In my experience the show goes on not by any laws of Heaven and Humankind, it just sort of finds a way. Come what will, by hook or by crook, in one shape or form, the cliché must ensue. My money says Roscoe's gonna make it.

Come soundcheck, the sun was warm and we were still minus a Roscoe. The rest of the band gathered around Leonard on stage as he shared his plan.

I listened in.

I didn't get it all, but surmised they had a duty to get on with things. Of one phrase I'm certain: 'They'll never get us.' That's how the show goes on.

An absent bass guitar leaves a gaping hole in the sound, but the band soundchecked anyway. By now there was a suggestion that Roscoe would make the show, so they didn't try anything fancy to cover for him.

The throne room

SHOWTIME

Of all my first-world problems, dressing up for the show is my bane, especially in warm weather. As zero hour approaches, restrictive trousers replace comfortable shorts. Time to wear the good shoes.

The audience are arrayed in ground level chairs and tiered stands. Many of them take to their feet and give Leonard a standing ovation when he jogs on stage — moments after Roscoe took position.

I have a pretty busy time during the show, tuning guitars, getting them ready for their appearance in accordance with the setlist. The only problem is Leonard deviates from the list at times. It pays to keep all the guitars constantly tuned, even if one of them is only ever scheduled once in the set near the end — because you just never know.

The show finished near the dot of midnight, four hours after Leonard took the stage. There was a 20 minute intermission, but still, over three hours of performing is pretty impressive.

Back to the hotel. Drinkies. Crew and band hung out. Finding myself alone for a moment I tipped a green bottle and emptied the last of its foam into my beer-chasm. It was then I saw, looking down the body of the upturned bottle, him.

Or rather his hat.

A wide brim, wreathed in smoke, edged around a corner.

Dupuis.

I shut my eyes tight, for I dared not steel them to his. First he finds your gaze, and so invited into your confidence he slithers to you and places a hand to your shoulder. I can almost hear his whisper: *Drink.*

'No,' I mutter.

Through a snowy hubbub of chatter, his caustic voice shivers a silence. *Drink.*

'I cannot.' My stubbled chin trembles and sweats.

Drink.

'You — can't make me!' I cried out.

Silence.

All eyes turn to me, a glistening wretch accusing an invisible enemy.

They're going to find out.

Opening night

August 13: Gent, Day Off

We've been working for six days. It's a laundry morning.

There's something you need to know about me. I have a weird thing with laundry. People who don't tour — muggles, norms, civvies, whatever — don't understand the joy of walking-distance-laundry.

It's a beautiful day today, perfect for a saunter to the laundrette. You get to pass by the *skull building*:

It silently judges me

The cobbled quay of Kraanlei leads to my place of worship. Bells are ringing. In my head. I remember this walk from 2010, the last time I was here. There's a curious little shop, and it seems to have become even more curious. Curiouser. It got supercuriosified. Its window dressing has changed, but the oddity remains. Multiplied even.

Two Ken dolls — two gay Ken dolls happily enjoying a moment, smiling at me, suggesting I was missing out on something. Perhaps they belonged to the

20

Experimental College Barbie range, I don't know. My thoughts turned to Barbie herself. How would she feel about clones of her boyfriend getting it on with each other?

The sex-mad icons can't have been thinking clearly — for one, the offspring of two identical Kens might be genetically deficient and secondly, don't they care about Ken's reputation? Do you remember Ken's friend Alan? He married Midge. Anyway, Alan is a total sports freak and he's the kind of passive aggressive jerk who'll orchestrate a homophobic bullying campaign that would ruin Ken's football career.

By football I mean what some folks call *American football,* with the squished ball and stunted episodes of men bumping into one another. A bit like rugby but shit.

Anyway I did my laundry.

Later I ambled around Gent, avoiding any moving vehicle that would cost anything to ride. I took in the town with a camera, noting colourful flowers made all the more vibrant by a deep blue sky. I bumped into Dan and Charley and had lunch with them.

Later in the afternoon I couldn't resist a beer.

I sat under a parasol and people walked by.

A young woman wearing flip-flops ambled along. She looked drunk.

'Hey.'

She turned to face me. One eye was bigger than the other.

I threw popcorn at her.

After dark, Paul and I grabbed a table behind the hotel and drank beer by the canal. The waterway was lined with tastefully lit buildings kept well over the centuries. Nearby an arched bridge of stone matched a great church.

A few beers later at midnight many of the aesthetic lights go out.

The canal is almost a mirror, reflecting delicate shimmers of streetlights onto the sawtooth continuance of buildings.

In the deepening dark, ripples become light wakes as a gondola drifts, manned by a figure cloaked in black, his eyes hidden by a wide brim.

A strong, stubbly jaw.

The figure lifts his head subtly, and thin lips part to disclose the unwelcome smile, an incomplete set of crooked teeth. He does not reveal his eyes, but raises his gloved hand slowly, fingers scissoring a cigarette. He clamps his lips around the butt.

He removes a glove, lightly tugging at each little sleeve, revealing a misshapen hand. His index finger is missing, replaced with a metal prosthesis which he flips open. A yellow flame hisses from the device and he lights his cigarette, the flickers casting devilish shadows on his features.

He puffs a chimney of smoke, his soul's windows hidden by a slick brim. Stiffly he raises an arm and points to me.

Dupuis, the Ghost of the Golden Hops, will reveal his eyes unless I make this beer my last.

Gotta go Paul, sorry.

Before Dupuis' arrival

August 14: Gent Show 2

This morning I awoke on a thin plane; like a tightrope walker I looked down into the abyss of a hangover but fortune touched my hand, guiding me to the edge. With the cobwebs clearing I got into a van and went to work.

A new toy arrived for my attention, a switching pedal to make Mitch's equipment a little simpler to operate.

TECH-YAWN TIME

Mitch uses three separate input cables for different instruments: electric, acoustic, and a Godin nylon-stringed guitar. Each cable is labelled appropriately for use. If all we ever did was rehearse, this triplet of lines would suffice but *heat of battle* rules apply. Cables can get tangled or worse, confused, creating an uncomfortable situation when the right guitar is played through the wrong audio channel.

This new-fangled pedal allows Mitch to employ a single input cable for all guitars, speeding up the song transitions and keeping the aesthetics sleek. I spent a little time this morning adapting the device to Mitch's pedal-board, ensuring ground loops were eradicated.

Mitch was happy with the new system and suggested a couple of changes simplifying the layout of his pedals. Tomorrow I'll make and alter cables, and reposition the wee dainty unseen things.

Wee dainty unseen things is tech lingo for a system of trade secrets involving cable-ties, tape, superglue, markers, hammers, chainsaws, blowtorches, inflatable dolls and Semtex.

YOU CAN WAKE UP NOW

The caterers made vegan pizza, vegan ciabatta thingies and one of my favourite pasta dishes, *spaghetti aglio, olio e peperoncino*. I'm going to be a fat bastard.

We saw spots of rain around 5 p.m., and at 8 the band took the stage under a thick mantle of grey.

Mitch enjoys the new pedal setup. We swapped guitars between songs and he said with a smile, 'This is working good!'

The rain stays up and Leonard finishes as close to the midnight curfew as he can. If he had his way, he'd keep playing 'until the wheelchairs rust.'

After the show we prepare the stage for expected overnight rain. Local crew staple a blanket of plastic sheeting to the stage while I case equipment.

I returned to the hotel as quickly as logistics allowed.

I bought a Hustler, scribbled a number on it, and shoved it under Chris' door.

I took a shower.

My phone rang and I put on a girl's voice. 'Ja?'

It was Chris. 'Um… hey, who's this?'

I laughed with a cutesy giggle. 'It's Inga, silly. You want hot times?'

Awkward pause.

'You want to make busy in Inga's skizzy?'

23

The Texan penny dropped. 'Leif I swear I'm gonna kick your balls.'
I doubled over laughing with tears and went to bed with a book.

August 15: Gent Show 3

I was the first of Team Backline to Sint-Pietersplein today because I had a little extra work. I needed to solder a few cables and arrange some dainty things.

I'm told today is the 250th show since Fredericton. It feels like a lifetime ago.

Weather radar shows patches of menacing red approaching us; it brings out the crazy in people's imaginations. We're expecting gusts of locusts and ham that will shroud the world in a living slime. The rain will tear your flesh from the bones.

We covered the stage with plastic sheets and watched the sky's eerie quiet.

After lunch I went for a little stroll for no reason.

I found a shop with a bunch of crazy antiques in the window. The guy inside wore a rain jacket and wellies.

He said something in Flemish.

I screwed my face up.

He pointed at me like I was a TV and he knew the answer on a game show. 'English!'

I just know this guy's going to chop me up. 'You got any old calendars?'

'Ships in bottles.'

'What?'

'I make good price.' He opened his jacket. His wiener was painted gold.

I ran out and barred the doorway with a chippendale.

Around 6 p.m., forceful gusts blew, swinging lighting trusses and speakers; there wasn't much rain, but enough to justify the plastic sheeting. After 15 minutes of bluster came a period of trepidation fuelled by talk of a second front. Thinking of band and audience, we took steps to ensure maximum safety, securing trusses and lowering video screens, effectively nailing down what we could.

The extra safety precautions are a bump in the daily routine. Breaking the flow can give people the jitters. You've seen it yourself — when it rains people forget how to drive. Some of us start to get a bad feeling about the gig, like something's not right. Not me.

If the wind picks up a grand piano and flings it at me I'll just get out of the way. I don't worry over the sky falling. I already know it is.

We started the show 30 minutes late to allow for the undoing of safety precautions.

Leonard is on fire tonight. He usually deviates from the setlist and brings it back on track but tonight he keeps us all on our toes, calling surprise numbers. As long as he and the crowd don't mind a little inter-song faffing (to get the required instruments into place) then I don't mind doing a camp power-walk on stage with a surprise guitar.

My favourite part of the day is not having to play dress-up. If the weather turns nasty I need the full power of shorts to spring out my inner ballerina and quickly batten down the hatches.

Apart from a few puffs of wind the weather held. There was no hurricane, tornado, cyclone, pack of wild dogs, earthquake, horse-flu or cloud of infected hypodermic needles, just Mother Nature's sabre-rattling.

I knew it.

This kind of self-confidence will one day bite us.

August 16: Gent, Day Off

So far this isn't a tour, but bear with me, we'll get going I promise.

In the meantime it's another day off.

I did laundry again. Ken and Ken were still getting it on.

I walked around.

I snapped some pictures.

Gravensteen Castle

25

Resentful robot cowboy

The height of excitement today was chips with mayonnaise. The vegan police have issued a warrant for my arrest but screw those guys. You can't be in Belgium and not have chips and mayo.

If potato issues confuse you, here's a handy table to help you translate while abroad:

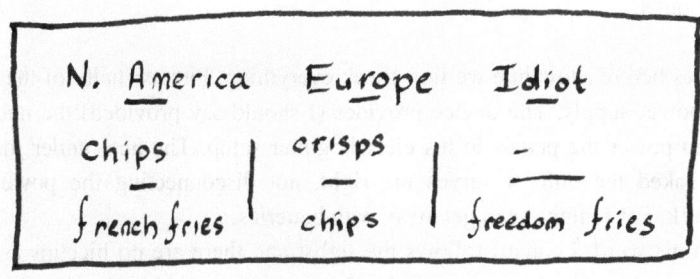

This is why we have days off.

August 17: Gent Show 4

Hotel breakfast doesn't interest me anymore. The same surroundings, same food, it all feels like a film starring Bill Murray. I skulked out of my room and found a shop. It's a peanut butter, wheat crackers, orange juice and banana morning.

Last night the local promoter Pascal took us all out for dinner. I waived the free booze. That's three nights of sobriety. It's tough to resist but everything is easier without a hangover.

Today's weather report: hot and lots of it. The outdoor stage is mostly shielded from sun but it's still warm in the wings. The sun drips lava onto the low ceilings and if it weren't for the occasional breeze it would be an oven in here.

TECHNICAL PROJECT: file down the nut slots in Javier's Fender Telecaster and lower the bridge a little. Nut-work is tricky. I didn't fuck it up.

Leonard performs a lone soundcheck under a big hot sun, working on some material. He and I chatted briefly about the last show, how wild weather and breaks in the routine have the power to unsettle.

'I hate it,' he says with a half-grin.

I guess we agree routine makes life simpler.

He tells me he's planning on sticking to the script tonight. I don't want him to know this pleases me. I'd prefer to keep up the mystique, that we can handle anything; in truth we like to know what song is coming next.

It's a fairly quick soundcheck. Even Javier the man from the deserts of Spain says it's hot. When the band are done we cover the gear with solar blankets and break for some quiet.

30 minutes before showtime we line-check everything. First casualty of the tour is Javier's power supply. The device provides (I should say provided) the necessary voltage to power the pedals in his electric guitar setup. The heat under the solar blanket baked the unit. It serves me right, not disconnecting the power after soundcheck. For tonight I can get away with batteries.

True to his word, Leonard follows the setlist and there are no hiccups as far as guitar changes go. He skipped a couple of songs to keep within the time limit, but it wasn't a hassle.

So Long Marianne is a crowd-pleasing staple of the set and outdoor audiences usually sing along. The people of Gent are high-spirited. Dubliners still rule. In 2008 the Dublin audience killed.

Mitch's new pedal, the one I raved about, yielded a scratchy noise. Otherwise the show was technically uninteresting.

August 18: Gent Show 5

THINKING

Gent is in the Flanders region of Belgium. I hope you're familiar with John McCrae's 1915 poem, *In Flanders Field.* Here are the first two lines:

In Flanders fields the poppies blow
Between the crosses, row on row,

I'm a bit of a history buff. 98 years ago to the month, the Great War began swallowing men in their thousands. That such a tragedy was until only a short time ago within living memory is thought provoking.

Soldiers of August 1914 said the summer was hot. Today in 2012 it's pretty warm, but we're lucky. We stand around in shorts on a covered stage discussing the trifles of laundry. In this temperature I can barely imagine sleeping with lice and marching for miles weighed down by the instruments of war.

YOU CAN CALL ME BOFFIN

Under the personnel list in the itinerary, I am jobbed as a guitar technician and *boffin*. At first I was unsure how to receive the moniker but after looking up the word I was happy with both title and its etymology. Wikipedia says:

> *"During World War II, boffin was applied with some affection to scientists and engineers working on new military technologies."*

I *boffinned* up a new lead using some low-capacitance cable which allows the guitar's *tone* to shine through. I hate when people use the words guitar and tone together. *My guitar has good tone.* Shut up.

The potentiometers in Mitch's switching pedal needed a squirt of contact cleaner.

Javier's power supply is screwed. The transformer is visibly dead. Skin of its insulated copper wire has melted, rendering the component irreparable by a lowly guitar tech me. With a 120-volt primary winding and eight secondaries, I'll have no luck in finding a replacement. I'll sooner discover a rooster with lips.

SOUNDCHECK

It's hot and soundcheck is brief. We powered down and covered the gear with solar blankets.

After dinner a few of us had a group power-snooze on stage left, either in garden chairs or atop any flightcase untouched by the sun. I woke up sweating in my cheap, uncomfortable folding chair.

Mental note: burn it.

Shortly before 7 p.m., an hour before showtime, word comes down from the boss that special attire shan't be necessary: avoid getting hot and sweaty, remain in comfortable clothes. I'd kiss him if I wasn't so gross.

When the sun lowered, twinkling behind tall trees above the last row of tiered seats, we uncovered the goods and got on with the show.

We started on time.

The set list is the same as last night's.

Tonight I noticed the quirky on-stage relationship between Leonard and Javier during the song *First We Take Manhattan*. Leonard kneels before Javier as if serenading him, speaking in a mix of verse and prose: 'I'm thankful for those items that you sent me.'

I can see Leonard's face, but Javier sits with his back to me. The Spaniard's arms and shoulders move in rhythm to his musical phrases; like a Juliet enchanted by a jukebox Romeo.

It's a complex relationship; mutual admiration is laced with theatrical mistrust. Toward the end of his serenade Leonard laughs conspiratorially, rising from deference. After all — he has practised, and now he's ready.

LOAD OUT

The stage-left dock is a bottleneck of cases going to different places, and truck-ramps have to be removed and repositioned frequently; the lane between truck and dock also serves as a forklift crossing. It's slow going but I don't care.

Paul probably hates it.

Certain folks are always in a hurry, they can't wait for anything or anyone.

Fuck you, be polite, you're supposed to be a professional. (Not you Paul, you're my favourite stage manager.)

One last look at Gent

August 19: Travel to Amsterdam

The crew left Gent at noon in a convoy of vans, an hour ahead of the band. The reason for this staggered leave is, I can only assume, safety. Should we encounter a deathly chasm, or Dutch highway pirates on the way to Amsterdam, the band and management will be spared the horror.

Some folks consider this a travel day but I call it a day off.

Amsterdam.

Evening-ish. I set out on a lone quest for food and met Ryan and Dan. My inner 20-year-old wanted to get hammered and amble through town wearing a conical hat, puking into canals. The reality of note-taking tells a sad tale. I had maybe four or five beers with too much Indian food.

My notes said this:

> *It's not what you might call fucked up, but I've achieved a level of cosmic incapacitation; I'm lying on the bed in my jim-jam shorts, praying to the food gods to take some of what's in me, out, so I can sleep tonight. I should know better, I should know better, I should know better.*

I should write for theatre.

Chris, bags, and an audience

August 20: Amsterdam, Day Off

Due to a concrete-hard belly I didn't sleep well last night. It feels like I ate a Dutch clog. I'll get over it, it's another day off in warm and sunny Amsterdam.

I wanted to wash a few items of clothing in the bathtub.

I rang housekeeping.

'Hello?'

'Yeah send someone up.'

'What do you need sir?'

'You got anyone good at staring?'

'Sir?'

'Staring contest. I can't wash my underwear unless someone's staring at me. There's ten euros in it.'

A short guy dressed in white showed up.

He blinked. I kept the money.

I went out for a stroll and found a chemist's.

A girl worked behind the cash register. Her face was caked in orange foundation and her lips looked like raw sausages.

I approached trying not to stare at her chest. 'Hey you got any hair dye?'

She pointed to the men's aisle.

'Nah, I like the chick colours.'

Her curled lip thought I was gay. She pointed somewhere else.

For most of UHTC it's not really a day off. Team Backline has the day to loaf but the rest of them are going in. Around 4 p.m., teams Production, Wardrobe, Audio and Lights shot out of town to the concert site, preparing for tomorrow.

There's no I in team.

All for one, one for all.

In it to win it.

Shut up. What would you do? Loiter in Amsterdam or drive to a stadium and hang around sweaty bodies pushing flightcases?

There's no line-check planned, so there's no need for us. We'd just get under the grown ups' feet. We'd feign courtesy by wandering around asking how to be useful and failing. It would be like asking a team of hairdressers to build the salon.

There may not be an I in team, but there certainly is in Team Backline.

August 21: Amsterdam Show 1

My reflection this morning had shiny blue-black hair.
Eat something.
Man shows up outside hotel.
We get in a van.
Today's set up was easy thanks to Saint Paul's efforts yesterday. He directed the unloading of the trucks and all our cases are sitting on stage waiting to be emptied. He also oversaw the laying of the rugs and the positioning of the risers.
It doesn't get much easier.
We were quick to set up. With the change of a few strings and a spike of an object or two, we're good to go for a line-check.
Today's challenge is the atmosphere. The weather is a mix of cloud and warmth, cool breezes and pockets of the undecided. The only constant is the humidity which makes guitars feel like they're sweating. One way to combat this sticky feeling is to polish the necks repeatedly; but polish is also a mild abrasive so be warned.
We're in a stadium. The stage is totally shaded so there's no need for solar blankets. Leonard and the band can soundcheck without the naked fire-eye glaring down on them.

Yeah I don't really get it

33

A 210-minute show is better than 240. The strict 11.30 p.m. curfew is a treat to us slackers in the wings.

Leonard has to cut a few songs from the set. My ESP is improving — there were no real surprises for me.

Javier is suitably ablaze tonight. During his solo at the beginning of *Who By Fire*, it was like he was possessed by Eddie Van Halen's Dutch spirit; he shredded the shit out of that archilaúd. Eddie Van Halen is still alive so I don't know if that's even possible.

The singalong favourite *So Long Marianne* is always placed at the head of the encores. Tonight the singing Dutch have trumped the Belgians, but the Irish still hold the cup.

Toward the end of the shortened encore, Leonard felt the squeeze of old Father Time. With six minutes remaining until curfew he thanked the audience, shared his blessings, and explained to them the temporal situation.

Moments later: 'Wait, it's only five now.'

After further thanks he caught himself: 'What am I doing, I'm wasting time!'

First We Take Manhattan began.

The dying moments of the show were unlike any Leonard Cohen gig I know of — zany — and I missed them.

I was just off stage, filling guitar trunks. I'm told Leonard picked up his clock (which sits at his feet, leaning against a monitor) and carried it around with him, 'cradling it,' according to Dan.

Leonard was no longer in command — time gripped the knife-switch while flowers flew on stage.

When the big hand touched the 6, the band ended the song professionally.

That was the end of that.

August 22: Amsterdam Show 2

Today is the last day in Amsterdam; after the show we travel by tour bus to Copenhagen.

I'm not sure if that seems strange, opening a chapter and immediately telling the end, but it's a habit we pick up on tour. The immediate future is a light at the end of a repetitive tunnel.

Most of the day is mundane.

We take things out of a truck, unbox and set them up, watch people perform, pack it all up, put it in a truck and do it all again, over and over. Light at the end of a tunnel is a reason to fight off the crazy.

Today is sunny, dry, breezy and cool, a perfect roadie day unless you're a sound engineer. Wind is a pain for them. But my world is perfect so screw those guys. No sweaty guitars, and the stable temperature makes for stable tuning.

I'm all about the little picture.

A glimpse of my mobile workstation

OUTDOOR POLITICS

Last night's curfew was in place at the running request of local residents who aren't fans of late-night music. Who can blame them, living near a stadium.

Saint Paul tells me something interesting; there were calls to the mayor's office apparently asking for the music to be turned up. So tonight we have a fifteen minute extension. Thanks a lot residents.

SHOWTIME

At 8 p.m., Leonard scoots on stage to a partial standing ovation. He signals for the start of the set: *Dance Me*. The standing settling into their nests.

Encores; *So Long Marianne* is impressive. It's a smaller audience than last night but they're stronger. During *Closing Time* the flock have fully fledged. They abandon their nests and crowd the barrier.

Leonard sings the signature line of the song: '*It's closing time.*'

The birdies cluck in response: 'No no no!'

The crew nod quietly: *Yes yes yes*. We want to get out of here.

THE ROADIE-FAN RELATIONSHIP

You have to understand something. Roadies earn their living from ticket sales. The experienced among us are aware we owe a professional existence to show-goers. But we become numb.

I can imagine experienced doctors and nurses — paramedics especially — having in-jokes about poisoning unruly or rude patients. There has to be a sense of humour behind the professionalism, otherwise they'd go crazy.

It's like that with roadies. We fantasise about whipping 9-volt batteries at punters who want us to down tools and run off to get something signed for them. Same goes for drunks who demand guitar picks, drum sticks, set-lists, *et cetera*. You paid for a ticket, you got entertained; you're not entitled to a free souvenir. Jog on.

My ultimate fantasy: We're playing in a small theatre; the front row is mere feet from the lip of the stage. It's the final show of the tour. When the show ends, people gather at the downstage edge demanding things. A few of us take the heaviest thing we can find, a B3 organ, place it on a wheel-board and with Monty Python violence in mind, gather ramming speed and roll it off the stage, crushing five or six people. We high-five each other and carry on.

It'll never happen but dear God I'd love to see it in a movie.

Penultimate fantasy: sitting on the edge of the stage and singling out an audience member, giving him or her the finger for the entire performance; for no other reason than solid, undeniable boredom.

Now you know two things: first, I'm an asshole. Second, although we depend on punters to pay our bills, we also see them as reasons we're away from our families for long stretches of time. We're actually pretty harmless, only slightly out of our minds.

BACK TO THE ENCORES

Time controls all. The band lowers its voice during *Closing Time* and Leonard sheepishly lifts his clock. He tells the audience the show must end. *Closing Time* is halted and *Save the Last Dance For Me* begins.

Two minutes to go.

Leonard replaces the clock and looks to Mike during the song, checking he's still within time's boundaries, going for it as long as he can, fulfilling his earlier promise to Amsterdam that tonight, that they were going to get, 'everything we've got.'

The minute hand hits 270° and the song is done.

LC thanks the audience; 'Good night friends, God bless.'

THE DIFFERENCE BETWEEN HUMBLE AND ARROGANT

Some artists think they can do whatever they want and play past curfew. Then they whinge when the local authority pulls the plug, even after reminders. *<cough!>* Bruce Springsteen.

By way of witness Chris I'm told that Leonard simply wants 'to be invited back.' And there it is: humility grants an extra 15 minutes; arrogance steals it.

LOAD OUT

As soon as the band clears off, the stage is awash with technicians, roadies, stage-hands, loaders, pushers, pedlars, prisoners, Chuck Norris and Godzilla, boxing the equipment, breaking down the risers and rolling the rugs. The trucks are 150 yards away; we push cases over soft track and cobbly bricks to get there.

After loading it's time to relax on the bus, our habitat for destruction. This bus has the capacity to sleep a dozen passengers, but we're only six tonight: Team Backline and Tom the merch man.

While we waited to go, Mickey and I destroyed two bottles of Champagne, gifts from Pascal.

August 23: Copenhagen, Day Off 1

I woke up in a moving bus. I can't wait to fall into a shower. I could've cleaned up last night but I preferred drunk. I'm only mildly hungover; Dupuis' yoke is but a ghostly chain-rattle.

We arrived at our hotel in Copenhagen around 2 p.m.
Our rooms were ready and Dave handed me an envelope containing a key.
Shower-laundry.

It's easier than searching out a laundrette, changing money (Denmark is kroner, not euro) and finding something to do between cycles.

What's shower-laundry you sick fuck?

Just step into the shower fully clothed and undress. If there's a phone in the bathroom you can mix it up.

I contacted reception.

'Front desk, how can I help you?'
'Guess what I'm doing right now.'
'Sir?'
'I'll give you a hint. I'm hot and wet.'
'I... don't...'
'Go on — and guess sexily.'
Click.

Nothing else happened.

This guy understands me

August 24: Copenhagen, Day Off 2

I went for a walk and got lost.

I found a Chinese all-you-can-eat and consumed enough for two.

With renewed legs I continued my search for the hotel.

I sat in my room and wrote.

Around 7 p.m. I'd had enough of my own company and went out looking for adventure. Just outside the hotel I bumped into Mike and Wade.

We found a pub.

Later on Mickey strolled in.

Around midnight a curious gust found its way in. It carried a faint whiff of tobacco. I heard something and straightened; a whisper, a murmur, an incomprehensible knot of breathy tones.

And I knew he was there.

Behind the bar he rose through the floor, his translucent form crystallising.

Dupuis.

He stood wrapped in a black cloak sheened like wet velvet. His head hung. That hat, his damned hat. Its brim shielded his eyes.

His voice is like swallowed sand. *Drink.*

I shook my head imperceptibly.

A gloved hand appeared from behind the folds of his shroud; with a subtle wave a trio of tequila shots appeared before Mike, Wade and Mickey.

That I see him is blessing and curse. The angels have armed me with foresight: a premonition of tomorrow's self-pity should I fall into Dupuis' abysmal stare. The curse is my enforced silence. The others will never believe me. Dupuis will torture them and I must watch, a punishment for my crime of preservation.

I had to turn my back and sacrifice my mates for sanity.

One is never saved from Dupuis' grip.

Exiting, I noticed a framed painting of an Irish poet; in its glass I saw my friends: leaning, listing on their barstools, enthralled in each others' tales. Dupuis opened his cloak and filled his chest with the drunken vapours of my colleagues.

Only in this reflection can I peer into his eyes.

And he knows me, leaving his corruption.

August 25: Copenhagen, Show Day

Today is the first of a back-to-back; two shows in two cities over two nights. For every other act I've worked with, multiple nights on the trot are standard practice; three to five consecutive shows in different cities is normal. But in Leonard Cohen world these days, back-to-backs are rare.

BORING STUFF ABOUT PACKING TRUCKS

This morning's project: document the backline pack. I came in early to study the goods as they were unloaded from the truck, snapping pictures of neatly stacked boxes in rows. I'll make line drawings noting how each item is placed and oriented. Then I'll write a list ordering the queue into the truck.

There's a good reason for this pedantic system. Backline is 3D Tetris. The boxes are all different shapes, and packing requires time and thinking. We're first into our truck and that means every minute we waste impacts everyone else to follow. Our goal is to fill space efficiently and leave a flat wall of cases; whoever's next has a clean palette to work from.

We're playing outside an army barracks. Behind the stage is the living quarters of young soldiers. They line up for inspection in their formal attire, topped by what appear to be bearskin hats.

If you stand on the outdoor stage and look out, Rosenborg Castle stands to your left. Looking centre, the green is flat and manicured; little vents exhale smoky gases of... something. Rain fell like a waterfall around 10am, but Mother Nature was kind after that.

Later on, soldiers marched up and down the square. I instantly think of the Monty Python skit.

Whistles, trombones, laser pointers, Glastonbury hats and bags of weed. They played a few marching tunes while Leonard was on stage soundchecking. I couldn't help but laugh. We're guests here; it would be rude to ask them to stop; which Saint Paul did.

And they stopped.

Reluctantly.

As they filed away, they banged their drums a few times. If it was in protest it's even funnier. That was the end of it.

TECH STUFF ALERT

Today's challenge was to build a new pedal-board for Javier. I acquired a suitable replacement for his burnt power supply but I need to make a cable converting a US *Edison*-type power outlet to a European *Schuko* socket. After doing that and refitting pedals, tidying up wiring, getting it wrong, taking it apart, and re-tidying wiring, it was all good and normal service resumed.

Maz's knee is a Blighty; she's being sent home to recover. If rumours are sound she'll need surgery. Her job is demanding; she has a lot of physical ground to cover, people to satisfy, and she does it well, never complaining, always ensuring everyone is looked after.

We'll miss her.

Touring life must go on, and we're getting a Tash. Natasha arrived late in the afternoon and will travel with us to Aalborg where she starts work for real in the morning.

Fact attack: Both Paul and Tash have worked for rock giants Iron Maiden.

The gates are open and people begin populating the green. There are no seats. The poor souls will have to stand on damp grass for hours. I can hear Mother Nature now (she's drunk); 'I'm gonna rain the fuck all over you because you worship Jesus and not me.'

She was mostly talk, it only rained a little.

41

Between songs Leonard requested the audience: 'May I draw your attention to the moon.' It hovered behind a yellowy haze in the darkening sky, and whether Leonard knew at that point Neil Armstrong, the first human to set foot on tonight's half-moon had only just died, I don't know.

Apart from that, for me tonight's show was much like the others.

Good night Copenhagen, good night moon.

Neil Armstrong got closer to the stars than any of us. Here's hoping he's at rest in the heavens.

August 26: Aalborg

My first bus-tour was 1995. It's not always easy to get a decent night's sleep on the bus and feel normal the next day. Being drunk helps you nod off, but the following day is difficult because you're a wretch. The secret is moderation. A couple of beers an hour before bed helps achieve a balance of rest and sanity.

I should mention Fritz our driver. He's a real German and that's his real name. His driving is smooth; not all bus drivers have the skill.

We arrived at the venue straight off the bus. As mentioned yesterday this sort of thing is normal for most bands, but with LC it's a rarity. We're accustomed to alighting spotless urban people-carriers, clean shaven, carrying man-purses stuffed with dainty machines and pens. The Aalborg venue isn't much more than a forest clearing. To stumble off the bus, white-knuckled and grappling a change of underpants is normal here.

The drive from Copenhagen should have got us here around 6 a.m., but the reality was 8 o'clock. Ordinarily this would be ok; we usually load in at 8 a.m., play at 8 p.m. But it's a 6 o'clock show tonight; we need to compress 12 hours' work into 10.

I got off the bus earlier than required. I do it for the breakfast. The catering tent must have been set up yesterday; everything in there was calm, unlike the flurry of action on stage to get the lights in the air.

I'm renaming Team Backline; from now you'll know us as *the Winning Team*. We are fortunate (and some hate us for it) to have it relatively easy. While some clamber from their bunks and head to the stage to discuss the mechanics of trusses and speakers, the Winning Team hangs around the food.

WORK EXPANDS TO TIME ALLOWED

For years I've known it, but it was only recently I learned the phrase. When time is tight the mind focuses. We clawed back the missing two hours and today becomes the usual clockwork of setting up backline, vacuuming the carpets, cleaning guitars, and even managing a quick lunch in time for Leonard's arrival.

After soundcheck Mickey looks terrible. There's something up with his breathing. He's taken to hospital for a scan and won't be able to work the show. The Winning Team are a man short. I'll be the only guitar tech on stage and if three guitarists need a change of instrument there's a potential for dead air. Thanks to Dan and Dave standing by we have enough bodies to perform a wholesale change if necessary.

SHOWTIME

The band hit the stage on time and the audience gives Leonard a standing ovation for the entire show; there are no seats. Tonight I have 15 guitars under my wing; they're a mix of steel and nylon strings, some six, some twelve. If Leonard sticks to the script, managing all the changes is foreseeable but fear of a wild card keeps me on my feet.

God's fiery testicle shoots sweat-rays on the stage. It's unwise to set guitars out there. That means almost every song I'm out there changing one or two guitars and by the middle of the first set I've seen a lot of action.

Temperatures begin to fall and guitars slip out of tune; checking and tuning often is crucial.

During the intermission we hear news that Mickey will stay in hospital overnight.

Our curfew is 10 p.m., but unlike Amsterdam where Leonard played to the last available minute, he ends the show a wee bit earlier so he can visit Mickey.

For most of the 210-minute show I was on my feet, tuning and re-tuning. One memory jumps out: when bringing Leonard's guitar to him and helping him get the strap over his hat he remarked, 'You're tall, good!'

43

LOAD-OUT

One man down, it took longer than usual to pack up, but people were cool. Normally I'd finish packing and get in the truck ready to receive the first row of equipment, but tonight my arrival is delayed until the third row. Thanks to Saint Paul and Shaggy the truck driver (he looks like the dude from Scooby-Doo) the backline cases are lined up and stacked ready.

AND BREATHE

We're staying in a hotel tonight. Once in my room I realised my entire night was like a whirlwind. I stood there pulling mysterious bits of paper from my pockets; days sheet, set-list, guitar notes, a receipt for a pound of blow.

I opened my clumsily-packed bag; it was a mess.

What the hell was I doing all day, why is everything so dishevelled?

Oh yeah, I was too busy thinking, worrying, and flying by the seat of my pants. In that hot room my world seemed in disarray.

'Fuck it,' I muttered and cracked a Danish ale.

I tidied my luggage and listened to music.

Hopefully Mickey will be ship-shape tomorrow.

If I had to really work for a living I'd forget to live.

August 27: Travel to Bergen

It's going to be a bus-day. I don't have to tape carpets to dusty floors, push flightcases around, lift this thing onto that thing, tune things, trip over things, yell at inanimate things, and do unspeakable things to things.

BREAKFAST OF KINGS

There's a meal your mom and dad didn't want you to know about. It's called *load-out food*. The caterers made me a to-go box last night and I saved it to eat in my room. It's a tub of hummus and a sandbag of carrots and cucumbers. It, and tea got me through the morning into the afternoon.

At 2.20 p.m., I packed up my stuff and checked out. The buses were parked outside, and I chucked my luggage into the bay.

I turned around and there was Mickey.

They kicked him out of hospital that morning after 'a full M.O.T.'*

He praised the quality of care and intimated that the nurses were sexy.

3 p.m., time to drive to Bergen.

There's nothing to do but eat crisps and drink beer.

When things calm down we watch the DVD screensaver and take bets on when the bouncing logo is going to hit the corner dead-on.

No one ever wins.

---

* *A Ministry of Transport certificate (MOT) is a yearly requirement for your aging car to remain officially roadworthy.*

August 28: Bergen

With the ferry ride It took around 12 hours to get to Bergen and when we arrived we parked at the gig.

I exited the bus to a wet and windy Norwegian morning. The floor of the outdoor stage is a patchwork of square plywood boards nestled in steel frames. Some boards are dry, some are puddled. We'll need to squeegee them before laying rugs.

If rain is fate we want it straight.

Fat chance; it's angular, it wants in. We put the rugs down methodically, laying plastic sheeting overtop as we went. Rain keeps us vigilant. No matter how new or professionally assembled these outdoor stages are, tiny holes and seams tend to leak a little. Leonard says there's a crack in everything.

45

We set up surprisingly quick. With Mickey back in the fold I have more time to ~~waste~~ reflect.

Like a burlesque show, the sun teased us from behind the clouds during soundcheck. The wind flapped the vinyl walls of the stage. Scaffolding and miscellaneous straps and buckles rattled and clunked. Mitch told me the distracting peals are like percussion played out of time. Soundcheck is brief.

THUS SAYETH THE BOFFIN

We're near a port; its communication matrix influences certain electrical circuits, namely the pickup in Javier's bandurria. A whine and low-frequency pulse renders the teeny-tiny guitar unusable. It falls prey to *RF*; radio frequency.

You expect electromagnetic waves to sound like a sine wave. The unwanted signals in Javier's guitar sound distinctly digital, maybe a mix of square and sawtooth, we don't know. Whatever the science behind the mischief, we call it *shit in the air*, or *RF*.

Fortunately we carry a backup solution: some acoustic putty sandwiched between the guitar's surface and a special pickup. You'd think we we're gonna blow something up. It allows the wee little guitar to be used.

46

No seats. Standing O all the way. During the first set Leonard called attention to a nearby tree. It seemed to him to move 'in absolute time to our songs.'

At half-time, in the distance behind us, a thick grey menace creeps through the sky. Patters of rain dance on the vinyl roof but we're spared a downpour.

With Mickey back in the lineup I had less to do tonight.

Naturally I made a boo-boo.

Have you ever thought you had all the time in the world to do something, and then suddenly time runs out and you wonder where it went? That.

I must've been under the impression that I'd left the correct guitar out for Mitch to grab, so I was equally shocked when he spun round to an empty stand.

His look of horror said *What are you doing to me?*

My drained visage said *Is this what death tastes like?*

Snapping into action — without looking like it — I sped on stage with the right guitar. What a schmuck.

Some guitarists wouldn't let you forget a mistake like that but Mitch is easy going, he lets go quickly. I guess as long as he knows I know I fucked up, that's good enough.

A few minutes before the 11 o'clock curfew, during the end phrases of *Closing Time*, Leonard said his goodbyes. I figured it was safe to begin stowing guitars. Packing stuff before the end of the show can be a dicey affair but everyone does it. Anyway the curfew is 11, what can he possibly oh fuck he's coming back on.

I Tried To Leave You.

Fortunately it didn't impact or reveal my jumping the gun.

There's no such thing as routine, only subroutines variously sequenced.

August 29: Halden

Back-to-back. Ten hour drive to Halden. Somebody threw darts at a map when planning this tour.

I awoke uncomfortably to curvaceous and bumpy roads; the bus roller-coasted between lakes and hills, accelerating, braking and popping wheelies in ear-popping plunges. When the road is winding and dynamic, you take your safety in your hands on a bus. You inevitably get jostled into something hard, pointy and immovable.

The upside is the scenery; handsome houses set in thick trees overlooking blue waters under a sky wisped with stretched cotton.

It's a double-deck bus, bunks upstairs, most other things below. There's a fridge. I opened it for a look despite its glass door. Suddenly the bus careened around a corner and as I grabbed the air for anything, the fridge vomited its contents. A boxed salad shot itself at me and I narrowly escaped its oily reach. Olives scurried along the floor like blind mice, hiding under leaves of slick lettuce. There's only one word, a mutter. 'Fuuuuuuck.'

I know what comes next and I'd rather it didn't.

Albert.

We rarely see him.

He's a three-foot-tall butler who lives in the luggage bay. He's a nasty wee shit but he has a thing for cleaning up. The last thing you want to do is disturb him. He speaks in sputters and hisses and once he gets going he ramps up the crazy until you feel as small as he.

Fearing his appearance I stooped and scrubbed the floor with paper towel but Albert smelt the mess. He shot in through a hatch, his patchy beard and wrinkled face grooved with menace. God I hate him but he's a wiz with floor polish.

I knew where this was going.

I recoiled. 'Albert, I—'

He punched me in the nuts and I bent like a sprung hinge.

Using silk napkins and myrrh he restored the tiled floor to a dazzle as my stomach lurched and my face streamed tears.

Fortune smiled on me; today Albert was keen to return to the bay. God only knows what he does there in the dark. With a final glare of twitching eyelids he made off, his thin hair floating in turbulence.

HALDEN

We finally got to the site around 1 p.m.

Fortunately the P.A. speakers and lights were hung prior to our arrival and it isn't long before the performance area of the stage is ready for carpets, backline and monitors.

Work expands to time allowed. Although five hours behind the normal subroutine, we raked back the time. On a normal day Leonard soundchecks at 4 p.m. and today we got him out for 4.45. And to think not one fist-fight, tar-and-feathering, shooting, flash mobbing or flag protest ensued in the rush. I even had time for lunch and some string-changes.

Incredibly, Mother Nature is kind. It's sunny, calm, cool, and dry; as a bonus the performance area is spared direct sunlight.

WHERE WE ARE

Atop a nearby hill stands Fredriksten fortress.

In a big house commandeered by our production team the local caterers have set up a posh dining room and Raf and I study a painting: in the background on a hill stands the fortress; below, houses burn; in the foreground troops retreat across a narrow bridge, harried by their enemies.

A young lady serving food told us more: the fortress was besieged in 1718 by Charles XII of Sweden.

So there.

SHOWTIME

You'll all be sore in the morning

No seats, those poor souls. I don't know how they do it.

In a surprise setlist change, *So Long Marianne* is uprooted from the encores and replanted in the first set. Leonard dedicates the song to the people of Norway, with whom he has a deep appreciation, citing specifically Marianne Ihlen.

That'll be the Marianne from the song I guess.

49

Wisps of cloud remain for the evening, and during *Waiting for the Miracle*, they part for the first star of the night. Leonard often shares his thoughts on how we are all 'privileged to gather in places like this,' while so much of the world is 'plunged into chaos and suffering.'

August 30: Gothenburg, Day Off

The bus rolled away from Halden in the dead of night and after maybe two hours' sleep I was awoken by — something — at 4.30am.

Albert.

Motherfucker standing on a child's step, swatting me with a rolled up magazine like I was a cockroach who wouldn't die.

'Alright alright, get off me!'

He hissed something and spittle flew between his teeth.

The magazine was Marie Claire; Rachel Weisz posed on the cover.

'Can I have that?'

Another voice entered the realm. 'You want to come with me to Stuttgart?' It was Fritz, the sarcastic German.

'No.'

Albert chuckled on Fritz's behalf. Bastard.

I grabbed a few beers, some vegan yoghurt, and the precious load-out food.

Suffering from bed-hair, I stumbled off the bus wearing underpants and steel-toe shoes. My luggage waited for me on the kerb. Albert stood nearby, grinning. Steam rose from my bags.

Scratching my belly I said goodbye to Simon who drives the other bus. It's filled with production and audio people, most of whom hate us. They hate the Winning Team because they're not on the Winning Team.

Dave met me in the lobby with my room key. 'What about your bags?'

I looked back. Albert's piss wafted off them. I grunted and took the key.

My room was on the 8th floor.

It was hot so I opened up the balcony door. The buses pulled away and Albert stood on top of ours, flashing his ass at me. It looks like a walnut shell.

I crawled into bed.

Around 10 a.m., I woke and hauled my body to the balcony. I haven't smoked a cigarette in ages, now would be a good time. The thought faded.

I looked below. In the circle of hedges outside the hotel entrance, I identified my strewn clothes.

I phoned the bellhop and asked him to go outside and gather my belongings. Watching him untangle my socks from the thicket, I figured he'd need a tip. I went downstairs, changed a fifty euro note into Swedish coins, and went back up.

'Hey!'

The bellhop looked up. His hat was jaunty, his face a criss-cross of thorn welts.

'You want some dough?'

He looked at me funny.

'I got you some money if you want it!' The first coin caught him off guard and he shouted something, but with the others falling around him he just got on with it.

My math isn't great but I figured I must have tipped him around 28 euros in kroner.

I don't speak Dutch or French or whatever, but he didn't sound grateful. Where I come from they say money's money.

Later the manager delivered my stuff. She had a black-belt scowl on her face. My handful of coins didn't cheer her up. She was taller than me; I figured she had the chops to fix me good, so I didn't say anything. She probably doesn't speak English anyway.

I took a shower and sink-washed some smalls.

I sat on the balcony and ate the yoghurt, some lentils and hummus, avocado, radishes, cucumber and parsley. Tea was good.

I caught up on the diary for a couple hours before heading out for a stroll.

There was a shopping centre nearby and I bought a black hoodie, some trousers and a faux-mink stole. I left my old clothes with the clerk.

I found a supermarket called Chinaski's. The lights were so damn bright I had to put on my shades. The store detective followed me around and stood behind me at the vegetarian food section.

I put tofu wieners in my basket and looked for mustard. Bread rolls and smoothie. I needed paper towels and baby wipes for work.

I picked up a tea towel and turned to the detective.

'Anywhere I can try this on?'

'Get the fuck out.'

'Good times.'

I ate in my room and wrote some fiction.

The tofu dogs and mustard were good.

August 31: Gothenburg, Show Day

This morning's hermit breakfast was peanut butter and wheat crackers, more of that vegan yoghurt and tea. We've returned to 'hotel-only' touring for a spell; for the next little while we're flying everywhere and sleeping in big beds.

BUS VERSUS HOTEL

Hotel touring: when leaving for a venue in the morning it's like you're going to work at a regular job. At the end of the day (which usually ends tomorrow) you return to a temporary home where all your stuff is sitting as you left it.

Bus touring: you fall out of a sealed metallic box into a dystopian future. The ozone layer is gone. You're temporarily blinded by the sun. You trip over your luggage and curse. You pat your hair down when good-looking people pass by. You walk around the block (the wrong way) in your pyjamas seeking an entrance to a venue with an unpronounceable name.

Bus touring has at least one upside, a certain simplicity. Travel while you sleep. Gods willing you arrive safely at your destination without subjecting your belt, laptop and shoes to a rectal examination. You don't have to queue up in an airport and kiss ass, look nice, nod politely, and gaze awonder at the idiotic processes humankind suffers, denying the terrorists have scored a tiny victory.

GIG

The venue is a little football stadium. It's a nice mix of outdoors and logistical support. The previous two venues had a distinctly rural feel, with tractors and generators providing various muscle. Here the manicured pitch is flat, much of it protected by grey plastic tiles. Goal lines flank the wings of the stage. A roof overhangs the stands, a bit like Rome's once-splendid coliseum sun-cover.

It's a bright and cool morning with a light breeze. Sparse clouds pass over, minding their own business.

By the time the Winning Team arrived the gear had been unloaded and we began unrolling carpets and assembling risers.

The local crew are young and inexperienced. It happens sometimes. Lots of people think pushing flightcases up ramps and lifting them over obstacles requires no skill whatsoever, but that's crap. Today's chaps need a lot of instruction, but we were all young once.

Again we're quick to set up.

Mickey points something out. It's a seated gig, and the ground-level chairs are padded with sponge and cloth. Comfy seat, but what if it rains before you sit on it? Not our problem, when's lunch?

The audio guys have their hands full today. The *slap-back* is almost unbearable. Echoes reverberate to the stage with every drop of a pin and it's difficult to tell at times which is the original sound and which is the carbon copy. There's nothing you can do about it, save draping the entire place in thick cloth.

When Leonard soundchecks, the previously undecided sky turns an adamant grey. If you were a critic you'd say it was living allegory.

Swedish caterers. Vegan bangers 'n mash. Too good.

SHOWTIME

The weather looks unpredictable.

During *Bird on a Wire*, Mother Nature decided to rain, but you have to give her credit for waiting until people were seated. She scratches the air with faint lines, pitter-pattering on plastic ponchos. Like the alliteration the rain doesn't last long.

No boo-boos for me tonight, my concentration is all there... most of the time. I can't resist the temptation of WiFi on my phone. As far as the show goes, you get to a point where your ears pick up more than your eyes. It's like spidey-senses; subtle nuances cause your ears to prick up and you search for something out of place. Otherwise you'll go blind watching the show all night, looking for disaster.

Under a clear sky the music stops. Our warm lights go out as cold stadium floodlights shine down. The metal-halide lamps are hooded, spaced along the edge of the oval canopy like Bernini's saints in the Vatican.

In the belly of the stadium's works there is a sweaty man, brow darkened by soot. He levers a metal handle beside a contoured fuse box and the floodlights awaken. He mutters to himself, having watched the show: 'That's how the goddam light gets in, now get this shit out of my stadium.'

We need to be quick getting out tonight because our truck drivers Super Steve and Shaggy have a long drive to Helsinki. Fortunately we only have the two trucks for UHTC gear — the lights and P.A. are local produce.

With the backline stacked in the truck, the Winning Team minces off site and back to the hotel.

Things have kicked off.

Queues for night clubs line the pavement, boy racers in the street over-rev their engines. We get out of a van looking like tramps compared to the dolled-up boys and girls out for the night. While clubbers clutch tiny handbags and cigarette packs, our hands are filled with day-bags, backstage spoils, and sacks of clean laundry.

September 2012

September 1: Travel to Helsinki

Dan; bags

We flew.

Apart from showing ID, pulling stuff out of my luggage, knocking back six beers and getting into a fight with a bartender, the travel was uneventful.

Helsinki was wet, grey and windy.

I got checked into my room and figured on a stroll.

Rain pelted my face as I leaned into the wind in a desolate car park. Finding a row of buildings I stuck to them. For a tourist, open territory is a dick-magnet. You never know when some gang of thugs is going to spot you out in the open and run you down like a stray cat.

I found a dingy supermarket with a yellow sign. A bell clattered as I opened the door and a woman behind the counter looked over her newspaper at me.

I shook off some rain and cleared my throat. 'You got any tea?'

'English?'

'What, me?'

'No, you want English tea?'

'I don't really care. You got green tea?'

She pointed down an aisle.

I found boxes of green tea. Each had a skin of dust. I lifted a box and drew a penis on the one left on the shelf.

'You got any tofu dogs?'

'What?'

'Forget it. How much for the bananas?'

I brought my own bag with me, a Leonard Cohen cloth tote, and it was drenched by the time I got back to my room. It was around 6 p.m.

Around 10.30 I lost interest in writing and phoned down to reception.

'Front desk.' It was a guy with an effeminate voice.

'What time is it?'

He took a moment to consider his answer. 'It's... ten-thirty sir.'

'Hey do you know if there's a nudie bar around here?'

'Sir?'

'A skin palace, strip-joint, diet brothel, you know, naked girls.'

A pause. 'Let me transfer you to the concierge.'

He covered the receiver with his hand but I could hear him talking to someone. I looked out my window and saw fireworks in the distance.

'Ah forget it,' I muttered and hung up.

The internet was too slow for porn.

September 2: Helsinki, Show Day

I chomped my lonely breakfast of wheat crackers, peanut butter and banana, and stared blankly to the outside world. Tree-lined side street and canal. There's a stone bridge of three arches and four lanes.

Another man with a van.

Another football stadium. We're playing down the field; the stage stands in the southern goal end. The pitch is a spongy artificial turf and in the blades of fake grass lie countless tiny plastic green balls. They get everywhere, I'm surprised they're not in my mouth. The weather says agreeable temperatures and rain isn't impossible.

Setup was another efficient process and I found myself twiddling my thumbs. In the itinerary it said the capacity of tonight's performance is 13,141. It seems so precise. I imagined some guy counting the seats and getting it wrong, how he'd feel knowing he had to start over again. I'd hate that job.

The Finnish audience isn't the most raucous, but they seem free-spirited. Early in the first set people danced in the aisles under a light grey sky. Here up north the sky won't darken until the intermission.

The only bump in the set was when Leonard called a surprise song: *Different Sides*. I bolted on stage nonchalantly to hand Javier his Telecaster.

That was the height of excitement for the day.

During the encores people crowded the barrier. In thanking the audience for their dedication, Leonard mentioned one Finn in particular, who, in '1995, when things weren't going so good,' started a website that breathed new life into Leonard's popularity. Leonard acknowledged the work of Jaarko Arjatsalo,* summing it up as a 'spectacular effort he's made on my behalf.'

A QUICK ONE... TO BE SOCIAL

The Winning Team is usually among the first crew members back to the hotel. When we arrived we saw the lobby populated by a few of the band and management.

Drinkies.

As time passed we were joined by further waves of crew and the place got busy with a UHTC drinking session.

A revolving door spun.

A dark figure entered, hunched, cloaked in black. Lidded by a sportsman's trilby, his leathery stubble stretched over a wide jaw. I sat perched on a marble window sill and the din of merriment wooled to a muffle.

Dupuis.

He stood behind the semicircle of our group. I am reflected in his empty eyes. There's no turning back, I am caught. Once his eyes are met his simple command must be obeyed: *drink*.

His prosthetic finger, tipped with a hissing butane flame points to the table before me, littered with glasses and bottles. The objects of Dupuis' minatory diktat are a set of shot-glasses and bottle of Finnish vodka. Like a powerless child forced by an elder to *wrong-do*, I reluctantly obeyed. Time slowed and the clear and soulless liquid fell into my glass. Inwardly I toasted nothing but my desire to break this grip, the stranglehold, the chain: the noose of the Ghost of the Golden Hops.

Amid the clamour of raised and drunken voices, Dupuis did his rounds. Standing over each intoxicated soul he filled his bony chest with the vapours of their drunken stupors. It is the aggrandised happiness of Humankind that feeds him; a jubilation to precede suffering.

Dupuis completed his parasitic nourishment and put a cigarette to his lips, lighting it with his burning finger. He pulled breath and exhaled smoke between his gritted teeth, gently squeezing the butt into an oval.

My head listed, engorged by the wit-slowing effect of his command.

He slipped away.

The phantom's cigarette smoke, the one trace remaining of his existence, swirled in the chambers of the revolving door.

When I could speak only in hiccups and my head bobbled atop a spongy neck, I managed by some primordial feat to find the elevator and my room.

* *Jaarko is the webmaster of leonardcohenfiles.com*

September 3: Travel to Berlin

I rose from bed around noon. I'm so hung the fuck over it's not even funny.

We're flying to Germany today.

I tried using the internet to check-in.

To my astonishment I discovered I'd already done it. Given how hammered I was a few hours ago I'm amazed I possessed the sentience to carry out the task. Maybe Dupuis did it. No, he's an asshole.

Rocco enjoys a snack in Helsinki

The flight left Helsinki on time at 5 p.m., and arrived in Berlin at 6. I was in my room by 7.

I needed Indian food. I found a place near the hotel and ate too much.

It's warm outside but not too bad. Dark clouds gather.

Cars speed by, their headlights begging to be stepped in front of. All of this could end with a skip off the kerb.

Girls are sitting outside cafés, giggling, toying with their drinking straws.

I look like Death's assistant, my pale face studded with hair.

A woman smiles at me sympathetically and hands me a coin.

'What's this for?' I burped uncontrollably.

She looked offended and took it back.

I got back to my room and thought about watching TV.

September 4: Berlin, Day Off

My hotel room overlooks a canal; strings of twig and leaf hang over its edge while sunrays shimmer on a rippling surface. The Winning Team have the day off. The rest of them are going to the gig to dump and fly their gear.

I brought my laundry to a *waschsalon* and a German lady took care of it. There was a language barrier so I yelled at her until she got the idea.

Dave says *Every day is a pay day.*

In my room I tried fixing Mitch's Godin guitar. One of the strings sounds quiet. Beneath the bridge there's a strip of piezo transducer thing. Strings make contact with the bridge, the bridge makes contact with the piezo and sound comes out through an electric pipe or something. I removed the bridge and sanded it, trying to make the underside perfectly flat. I replaced it and there was no change in the defect.

I scratched my head for a minute.

With my trusty hammer I banged the shit out of the guitar.

I took it to Mitch's room in ruins.

'What happened?' He wore a look of horror as I handed him a shivered remnant.

'Shit. Shit happened.'

His eyes were slits. 'I'm gonna get you for this.'

'No you're not. Roadies always win.'

We stared at each other. A maid appeared. She looked at us funny and got in the elevator.

'You wanna get some dinner?'

'Just ate.'

'Whatever.'

Every day is a *payback* day. Mitch has never done anything bad to me, but there's always the previous life.

I went to a Chinese restaurant. Tofu and veggies.

September 5: Berlin, Show Day

A pair of tour buses appeared outside the hotel.

Trees reach to a pale gloom.

Today we're in the Waldbühne, the Forest theatre. It's a steep amphitheatre, apparently a reproduction of a theatre in the ancient Greek city of Epidaurus. The Waldbühne is part of a larger plan, the Reichssportsfeld, built for the 1936 Olympics. If the '36 Olympics were a vehicle for nazi propaganda, it's easy to imagine the ghost of Goebbels haunting this place. Supposedly Hitler had a box here and spoke on this stage.

Upstage centre, you can access a concrete tunnel built into the earth. It's a zig-zag procession like communication trenches of WW1, of which Hitler was a veteran. Local knowledge says the tunnel was built this way so you could escape a bullet.

The morning rain seems light, but before you know it you're soaked. Moving on, it left behind a dense humidity. Shortly after noon the sultry air was burned away by a shy sun and hungry mosquitoes wanted lunch.

The backstage area is a hamlet of aluminium-framed tents with wooden floors, and sea containers variously repurposed. Walking uphill over rough cobbles toward food, I ponder the trees. I wonder if they have opinions, on nazis, on the madness of crooked men's dreams unfolding.

The king of kutlery doesn't care

SHOWTIME

Around the fourth or fifth song I realised how high the stage is. It looks like eight or nine feet above the ground level seating. There's no need for a crowd barrier, only an undulating plastic chain. Surely it would take a madman to scale such a height, to sit in an unassailable position.

I love the idea of Hitler fuming while a jew sings on his stage.

During *The Darkness*, infinite camera flashes become stars in the fading daylight. After *Going Home* came an extended applause. Leonard removed his hat and bowed humbly.

The Partisan; Leonard's adaptation of *La Complainte du Partisan** is a song of French resistance to nazi rule. In France, audiences thunder and roar after the song. How does it fare in Deutschland, the former bully of Europe? Unanimous approval.

So Long Marianne opens the encores. Berliners are loud. Angels in the audience wave white-hot sparklers. They all want to hear *First We Take Manhattan*, and they're on their feet. The chorus of, 'Then we take Berlin' brings down the house. It's *Bundescohen*.

* *Written in 1943 by Anna Marly and Emmanuel d'Astier de la Vigerie.*

63

Waldbühne

September 6: Mönchengladbach

Mönchengladbach, Warsteiner Hockey Park. Never heard of it.

News on everyone's lips is the unrest in Lufthansa. Are they going to strike? We're supposed to stay in a hotel tonight and fly Lufthansa tomorrow to London. Do we trust them, or do we cancel the rooms and take the buses?

At the moment the airline hasn't cancelled the flight. If *we* cancel, we might not get a refund. It's also too late to cancel the hotel and expect a refund there.

It's up to the production team to make a decision.

We're a little late this morning. The upside is the P.A. and lights are all the same as last night's gig. It's not too long before the stage is ready and the Winning Team can do their thing.

We stole back the time.

The decision is handed down: we're taking one bus to London, Simon's 12-berth. We're a crew of 17 so we have to donate 5 people to the band party who travel separate.

Hard curfew tonight. It should be like a steam-whistle after a day at the crap factory. Supposedly 10.45 p.m.

The show is scheduled for 7.30.

For whatever reason, we're holding for ten minutes. As if by magic the curfew was extended. We sulk like schoolchildren: we just want the bell to ring so we can cram our shit into a desk and bugger off.

The show happened.
Around 1.30 a.m., Simon's London-bus was packed with people looking forward to Blighty.
It's a mixture of the Winning Team and the rest of them. Most of the others hate us for various reasons. We're like the mailroom guys who've somehow wangled an invitation to dine at the boss' table.
They stay up late arranging things.
We show up and polish guitars.
It's the same on every tour. Backline guys are the hate-focus until someone needs a fuse, or a plug adapter for their shaver, their headphones fixed, their bags carried, electrical current or capacitance explained, or some free guitar strings.
It'll never change so there's no point in us trying to win respect. We're the Winning Team and we win in subtle ways.

September 7: London, Day Off

We arrived at a UK Border inspection station near Calais around 4.30 a.m. I wandered groggily through officialdom, met by a red-faced man behind a podium. He was slightly rotund, wearing a grimace.
'Good morning,' I muttered.
'Passport.' He leafed through my Canadian booklet.
'Hey check page six, there's an IDL stamp.'
He peered at me through his eyebrows.
I yawned.
He squinted at my *indefinite leave to remain* stamp.
'How did you obtain this?'
'I banged Thatcher.'
'What?'
'What?'
He shook his head and stamped me in. They always do.

BUS RULES

If your bus drives into the belly of a ferry you're supposed to get out and join the happy ranks of holiday fuckwits above. Legend states that vehicle decks are sealed off before sailing, and if you're in the bus while the ferry sinks, you'll be found some time later, bloated and grey.

It's 5 a.m. and I don't want to get on a bloody ferry. Thankfully there's a god for that; we're taking the Eurotunnel.

If you call it the *Chunnel* you speak like a dirty person.

I recall, sleepily, the bus driving onto a big empty train car. I recall a short and smooth journey under the English Channel. Arriving in Kent, the dream state was chipped away by a bumpy, twisty affair.

Fact attack: when you're in a bunk you lie with your feet pointing in the direction of travel. In the event of a sudden stop you prefer broken legs over a snapped neck.

The drive from Kent to London always feels like an uphill affair; with feet forward, the bus roaring along an interminable incline, your head fills with blood. Sleep is difficult. This drive is usually spent awake.

Around 10.30 a.m., we alighted the bus in central London outside the exclusive Landmark Hotel on Marylebone Road. It's tacky. The covered piazza of chairs and tables reminds me of Vegas. A continental breakfast is 25 quid and includes a man playing nameless tunes on a grand piano. It's all fitted suits, polished shoes, and skirts below the knee. Even the maids look a damn sight more cultured than I do. My broken luggage and faded black clothes lower the property value.

The band party (and five specially selected crew members) are flying here in a chartered plane, and should arrive around 3 p.m.

Our rooms aren't ready.

After a quick bowl of cereal and some orange juice generously invited by Dave (I hope that didn't cost £25) I went for a stroll.

ETYMOLOGY

Everyone pronounces Marylebone as mar-lee-bone. But look at it. If you pronounce it phonetically, it's Mary-le-bone. It took years of driving up and down this road to spot the curiosity.

I dug up some facts. *Bourne* is an Old English word for small stream.

There was once a church called St. Mary's near a small stream. There's a bit more to it, but it's essentially Mary by the bourne, Marylebone.

I came across Baker Street — it's not just a saxophone song — and did what every tourist does; bought deodorant.

I went back.

Still no room at the inn.

Some of us got rooms, some are milling around. For hours I tapped laptop keys and watched rich people eat their money.

There's a conference about Africa's pension and sovereign funds.

I can't take much more of this. If the flying party arrive and get their rooms before me, I'll question the validity of everything.

3 p.m., the band were almost here.

I finally got my keys. I think some hotels make you wait on purpose.

This is a posh place and I guess posh people don't like fresh air, afraid they'll catch a death on the wind. My room is stale. Spacious to be sure, but hermetically sealed. Maybe the super-rich get windows facing Marylebone Road.

My room looks over the sterile piazza, a mundane vista of people eating.

I imagine the sight of people-eating; eat the rich baby.

Trapped in an alabaster limbo

September 8: London Show 1

The atmosphere is stressful today. God I hate London shows. No matter the band, the higher-ups always regard the London show an 'important' one. Same goes for Los Angeles, New York, Tokyo... Just when you get into a good rhythm, when things are going well, when the useful subroutines are established, someone up the chain says *important*.

The word filters down the group's nervous system into the Hands, people like us who move things, tape things, set things up and hope to make things look nicer than usual. We feel pressure to do things differently all of a sudden, because it's 'important'. It's bullshit.

We're not dummies; we know there are certain geographical concentrations of movers and shakers in the music bizz. If this were an up-and-coming band of twenty-somethings you'd expect some trepidation and hand-flapping in the lair of the beast. But Leonard is a seventy-something guy with a backlog of achievements, playing to a five-figure audience. The man has already arrived for Christ's sake.

Do we think the London audience is more sophisticated than the audiences of Gent, Amsterdam, Copenhagen, Aalborg, Bergen, Halden, Gothenburg, Helsinki, Berlin or Mönchengladbach? I think it's an insult to say London is more important. Each show should be as important as the first, the next, and the last.

Despite loading in at 6 a.m., the audio department faces technical issues. Installing a stage left wing for Mickey and I has stripped a chain-hoist's power cable. The issue has a hint of irony: the hanging of the delay speakers has been delayed.

FACT ATTACK

If you're in the cheap seats, sound takes longer to reach you than it does the people at the front. Some speakers are placed closer to the cheap seats to effectively boost the sound. The signals to these speakers are electronically delayed.

Electrical signals travel faster through copper than sound travels through air; if there was no electronic delay, the cheap seats would actually hear the delay speakers before the distant speakers at the stage. In practice, there would be a constant delay, or echo, or *phasing* of the sound. Life in the cheap seats would suck.

Okay, so Mickey and I are the villains. Without the wing, the audio guys wouldn't have this issue. But if we're five feet below the action, we can't see much, and if we need to get out there in a hurry, we waste valuable seconds in dead air. And you wouldn't want that in an *important* show, would you?

By the time we laid carpets, built risers, set up and cleaned the instruments, line-checked, tidied the lighting and audio cables, vacuumed the rugs, scrubbed the chalk-marks off the stage, pulled up old tape, got the water and towels, and crammed every possible piece of *et cetera* into the 'important' show, the stage was show-ready. We aim to have it in a state of calm and readiness for Leonard's arrival.

All is not calm out there beyond the stage; soundcheck is delayed because of drapes, or lack thereof. In bigger venues the acoustics are aided by hanging drapes which soak up unwanted reverberations. At the cheap-seat end of the hall, the drapes are missing and the audio guys have pulled hair out, barking up a departmental tree for hours now. It's the venue's responsibility to hang the drapes — it's a 'house thing'. With time becoming a squeeze, soundcheck went ahead without the drapes. Happily by the end of soundcheck, stress had left the building.

SHOWTIME

We were looking forward to the 7.30 p.m. show and 11 o'clock curfew. At 7.20, our pre-recorded notice went out over the P.A.: 'Ladies and gentlemen, the show will commence in ten minutes.'

Fact attack: that's Dan's voice.

Seconds after the announcement our radios told a different story. We're holding the show by 15 minutes with a curfew extension.

At 7.40, more news. Show starts at 8.

The crowd begin to grow restless and so do we. If this were an Axl Rose show, the O2 Arena would like *The Day After*.*

The problem rested with ticket handling; by 7.30 there was a big backlog of people waiting to get in. This wasn't a case of *should have got here earlier*, this is a technical issue with the venue.

Moments before 8 p.m., the band take the stage and open with the usual *Dance Me*. After the song Leonard apologised to the audience for the delay, the change in venue, and the associated costs and inconveniences befalling many audience members. We were originally scheduled to play Hop Farm in Kent, not Wembley.

'I learned the same time you did,' says Leonard, rousing the audience into laughter. Apparently the decision to change venues was made without consulting him. He said it was made by people whose 'hands I never get to shake — or crush.'

Those 'important' movers and shakers literally live up to their titles. Many people had to change plans at considerable cost to come to Wembley.

Once we get going it's a pretty smooth ride — although I went on stage to change guitars without my hat on. I've never done that before. Then it was Mitch's turn. While I stood behind him, waiting to swap guitars for the next song, he carried on with the 'wrong' guitar. By the time he noticed it was too late, but we shared a smile.

That's the pressure of the London Man. That hidden Man, that faceless moving-and-shaking Man, he who thinks his house is more important than a hockey field or a town square — God damn that pusher-Man.

*The Day After *was a 1983 American TV movie about nuclear war. It caused a lot of interesting controversy.*

70

September 9: London Show 2

The view from the cockpit

A man with a van took us to Wembley. For as long as I can remember I thought Wembley was the name of the venue and no more. Turns out Wembley is the name of the area; who knew. Through the magic of Wikipedia I discovered Wembley was a village known during King Henry VIII's days. Going further back to the year 825, it was known as *Wemba Lea*, two Old English words. *Wemba* was simply Wemba — a person's name. *Lea* means clearing. Wemba's Clearing. Wemba Lea was part of a parish called Harrow on the Hill; the hill's significance stretches back to pre-Christian times.

There was no stress today. No load-in, no pondering, no interminable rumination of multi-layered solutions.

SHOWTIME

Again the show is delayed by 30 minutes. Again a problem with tickets. I was told the Hop Farm tickets were valid for Wembley, but Wembley also printed their own. With two types of ticket to authenticate, I guess things got slowed down.

Similar to last night, Leonard made his apologies and sought to assure the audience: despite what rumour suggested, the venue change wasn't his decision.

71

He shared a desire; from now on, he should inspect the hands of such decision-makers for calluses.

Since yesterday's entry discussed at length the philosophies of *importance*, I neglected to mention the stifling temperature on stage. It was hot and sweaty all day. This afternoon however, the temperature was agreeable. Now during the show, it's ass-hot. Bloody venue managers. They should check out this new-fangled device; it's called a thermostat.

LOAD-OUT

The gear is ramped off the stage and into a nearby truck. The Winning Team are finished in a tour record 48 minutes.

The 'important' shows are done. We survived the inheritance of pressure and overcame the dales of theatrical adversity.

Our harrows on this old hill are behind us.

September 10: Travel to Dublin

I'm saying goodbye to opulence, exclusivity and luxury, stirring steeply-priced tea with a sterling silver spoon. We're leaving the Landmark, where guests' pocket money is the staff's stretched paycheques; we're going to Dublin for the *craic*.

Fact attack: craic is an Irish term for fun and merriment. If you're completely *blootered* on Guinness, gleefully stumbling between tables to the tune of a penny whistle and *Follow Me up to Carlow*, you're experiencing the craic.

In this business you essentially travel for a living; you get used to being in different places. But for some folks Dublin yields the trepidation of an Antarctic mission. Irish weather seems to instil a kind of neurosis. The grey, the drizzle, the cold nights, these are the things that go bump in the night for some.

They go into a tizzy of forward planning; because you see, you can't buy warm clothes in Dublin. It's the last outpost of the former British Empire; bandits and cut-throats are everywhere; the interminable fog dampens your screams. Paymasters and shylocks prowl the mist offering passage to New Delhi, delivering you only to the vivisectors.

It's not the bloody Wild West, it's Ireland for feck's sake.

When I was growing up my friend used to fuck with his American pen pals: 'Exciting news, we just got a new horse and cart.'

The ride from Marylebone Road to Heathrow was unusually quick.

The x-ray queues were light.

The 2012 Paralympics are over and the terminal is peppered with competitors. Wheelchairs are common. Prosthetic body parts with luggage tags.

Some of us had good breakfast.

This is all going smoothly, where's the daily Hell?

The flight is delayed; ten minutes they say. It sounds like airline bullshit. 'Ten minutes' usually becomes 20, and so on.

The delay was around an hour.

I can't really complain because it's the Winning Team's day off. The others will go to the gig to load in, doing what they can in advance of tomorrow's show.

Elaine met me in Dublin. Without the kids.

It's a school night so it would be a bad idea to overdo the booze.

Around 11 p.m., Elaine and I were pounding back some beers in the bar beside the Gresham Hotel.

Suddenly I experienced a kind of imbalance, one of my ears becoming less adept at its function. With the distraction came a dull ring and somehow I was compelled to turn my head.

A cloaked figure appeared in the doorway, slyly, beneath a wide and dusty brim. The rough-faced brigand confidently exhaled a plume of smoke from a cigarette he ended on the pavement outside. With an affected grin (for he knows no happiness) he fixed his empty eyes on the vessel in my hand. The glass grew heavy once more. Dupuis.

Elaine does not see him; she knows nothing of this demon. Her voice in my ears is a wooly parlance regarding an event in which I cannot take interest.

I am paralysed by this devil.

He need not enter, only watch.

He has fed elsewhere this night, he comes only for sport.

My eyes filled with shaking want, I plead for him to stay this wanton violence. I am a quivering-lipped wretch and he is the master.

His menacing smirk widened, revealing a spectrum of grey and yellow gravestones.

This is the day's Hell visited.

September 11: Dublin Show 1

Elaine is heading home to Larne. She'll collect the kids and return tomorrow. Thanks to Dupuis I'm hungover like hell. *Not on a school night.* I'll keep telling myself that.

Today is going to be a mental hellfest. Hangovers are unprofessional and can pose dangers to others. Who am I kidding, this is the music business. If I had a euro for every time I showed up to work reeking of alcohol, I'd have a free suit.

I don't do this sort of thing often these days, but in 1995, oh my God.

On days like this achieving a bare professional minimum is the best you can hope for.

We're at IMMA, the Museum of Modern Art, Ireland. The former Royal Hospital Kilmainham has been repurposed for works of, you know, art.

There's a constant wind; decorative flags flap and snap. It might rain, it might not.

Thanks to the efforts of yesterday's comer-inners, the carpets were laid and the risers placed. The backline was on stage and with the help of some jolly stagehands, after an hour or so the place looked like a Leonard Cohen show.

What I did for most of the afternoon, I don't know. Probably sat down a lot and moaned about a sore head.

SHOWTIME

There was a downpour at some point today and by showtime the wind lessened considerably. The sky was screened grey-white with expert upturned strokes. It was like angels used hair curlers as brushes, drawing thin white wisps on a blue palette. The scent of barbecue shot across everything.

If you've ever worked a repetitive job, you'll know what I mean by *autopilot.* You don't really think about what you're doing because you've done it so many times.

When the band hit the stage I have a small panic attack.

I have no idea how I got everything up and running.

It was like the day just kinda happened around me. I ran through a chaotic checklist in my mind, wondering if I did everything necessary to ensure all precautions had been taken against folly.

Thankfully this self-doubt is a psychosomatic side-effect of Dupuis' cruelty. Autopilot did its job, everything was ok.

Dubliners give Leonard a standing reception upon his entrance, but as the set progressed they seemed quiet compared to my memory of our last visit here.

By the second half of the show I started to feel normal. By that I mean only partly dreadful. In the damp cold the crowd began to warm up. I think beer had something to do with it.

Hallelujah; a man in the audience has a personal epiphany. He stands up wailing along and I can't help but laugh. Dupuis will feast on this guy's vapours later.

Take This Waltz; loads of people are dancing three-four in the aisles. And then the stewards and security guys have to get involved, trying to get them all to sit down. Why, is beyond me. The dancers only multiply. People like to have a good time, and when no one's getting hurt it makes authority look all the more foolish.

So Long Marianne doesn't disappoint — just as well, considering the smoke I've been blowing up the Dublin crowd's skirt since Gent. The crowd preempt the choruses, rally along and Leonard acknowledges them: 'You sing so pretty.'

During choruses of *Famous Blue Raincoat* the people sing softly together. I get goose-pimply.

When people speak with one voice I think maybe one day we'll all stop being dicks to each other. One day we'll overcome the authority that demands we sit down and watch.

I don't know how, but I did my job today.

September 12: Dublin Show 2

Sometime today Elaine and the kids will arrive and set up camp in the Gresham. I'll be at work.

The Winning Team get in a vehicle that was neither van nor bus but something in between. We alight at IMMA, where a block of six portable cabins make up our production area. A couple hundred yards away, the stage stands like a remote castle in the constant wind.

Approaching stage left by way of aluminium panels acting as a temporary roadway, you're met with the sight of an obelisk some two miles away, north. It's Phoenix Park's Testimonial of Wellington. I heard yesterday that the Duke of Wellington is a disliked figure in Ireland. Why not pull it down if the guy offends?

Field Marshall Arthur Wellesley, 1ˢᵗ Duke of Wellington was born in Ireland, but locals say he wanted to be remembered firmly as British. Apparently he said something like *Being born in a stable does not make one a horse.* With that you'd suspect Wellesley fits the stereotypical mould of a British official harbouring disdain for the Irish. But — as prime minister of the UK, Wellesley worked for the *Roman Catholic Relief Act 1829*, allowing Catholics to sit in Westminster. Apparently he even threatened to resign if King George IV didn't give Royal assent.

From that, Wellesley doesn't strike me as someone who hated the Irish.

During tonight's show, Mickey asked me, 'Do you know who's here?'

I didn't know.

He pointed out a red-scarfed, happy-looking guy in the front row. 'The president of Ireland.'

In the encores the *prez* is protected from waltzers by arm-linked guards who are surprisingly indistinguishable from other security guards. Where are the thugs in suits who speak into their sleeves?

Following a quick pack-up after the show we returned to base.

The kids were in bed and Elaine and I crept downstairs for drinkies.

September 13: Dublin, Day Off

Ha'penny Bridge, spanning the Liffey

The Bodnarchuks exhausted themselves with walking, shopping, and eating. When you're separated from your kids for weeks on end, you want to buy them some crap. They'll leave Dublin a little heavier than when they arrived.

'Why are we getting this stuff,' asks my son.

'You don't know what day it is? It's Saint Brooklyn's day.'

'Who?'

'Saint Brooklyn. Nephew of Jesus.'

'Jesus had siblings?'

'You talk too much.'

It was amazing how quickly disbelief gave way to material possession. And now the devils expect a day off school and gifts every September 13 for Saint Brooklyn's day.

We ate dinner at the Hard Rock. The kids aren't sophisticated eaters, and if they can chow down on chips while Mummy and Daddy bang a few Mojitos, we've reached the nirvana of parenthood.

One Winning Team member had an experience beyond the usual day-off-wander. Chris adventured outside Dublin's sphere and bumped into artist Jim Fitzpatrick. There's a good chance you've seen Jim's work. You know that monochrome thing of Che Guevara? That was Jim.

September 14: Dublin Show 3

I took an early van and worked in solitude, changing some strings and generally pottering.

The wind is constant. Gusts shake the stage, squeaking its frame and rattling buckles. Even in the outdoors I begin to feel a cabin fever.

I saw grey figures float through the lake of folding seats, wandering in search of something. 'Hey!'

A ragged woman turned to meet my gaze. Her cobwebbed face was pocked, her matted hair hovering like twigs. Her mouth moved but I heard nothing.

'You want a set list?'

A gossamer child sprinted through the chairs and the woman turned her head to him. She shrieked in chase and they both vanished.

I sipped a Pepsi.

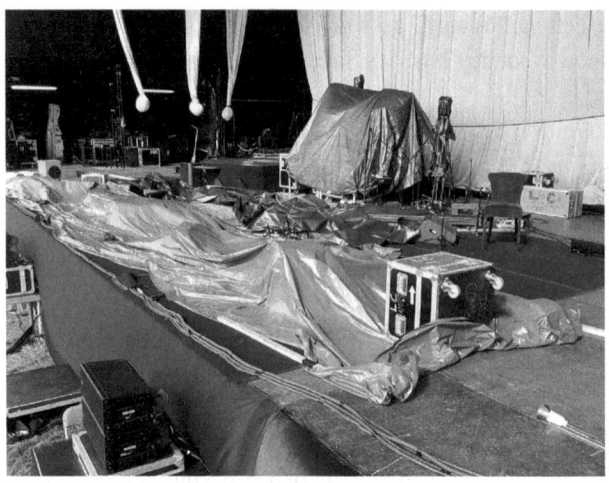

This is where the magic happens. So magical.

Of note this evening Leonard sang an *a cappella* verse of a song I'd never heard before. The memorable phrase went *Let my people dance.*

Sung moments before *Take This Waltz*, it sounded to me like a request to the venue's security staff: lay off the dancers.

September 15: Dublin Show 4

The cookie-cutter days draw to a close with the final show in Dublin. Each day the decorative flags flatten themselves in wind headed south; spots of rain fall and temperatures carry a confusion. The sun takes its cues from *The Karate Kid.** When it pokes through the clouds we layer off. When it retreats behind them, we layer on. Layer on, layer off, *ad infinitum.*

A surprise addition to tonight's set is *Anyhow*; it's well received by the audience who revel in their own bawdy responses to the ambiguously raunchy number.

It's been a while since we packed everything up and put it in trucks.

It's been a while since anything happened.

*A 1984 movie; a young man learns Karate through the power of montage.

September 16: Dublin, Day Off

Signed by who?

You're probably wondering why we're still here. You'd think we'd get on a bus and scram, but not this tour. We're flying to Istanbul — tomorrow. Usually a tour favours moving on, but we're opting for the extra day.

My notes said this:

Tired legs, little sleep, worn out in general. Family things.

Trying to balance family and work on the road is difficult. To ordinary folk we roadies seem to lead interesting lives; Elaine's colleagues ask why her husband doesn't take her with him. The road is a stressful place for family life, unless perhaps you're the Partridge Family, and everyone is working, and there are sufficient hours set aside for family time. The road offers a near-iron ultimatum: all or nothing. On work days it's hard to do anything other than work.

'When do you finish?'
'When the truck doors shut.'
'When's that?'
'I don't know.'
'You must have an idea.'
'Yeah but if I tell you, you'll hold me to it.'

I don't know if a forklift is going to break down, if all the local crew are going to turn up, if someone on our crew is going to throw a hissy fit, or anything else. You can guess, but nothing's ever concrete. No matter what, you get pulled this way and that between a demanding job and trying to please your family.

Around 1 p.m., I waved goodbye to my people in Connolly Station. It was a fun but exhausting visit.

I pottered about the shops. I like the weather: sunny, rainy and sunny again.

Only hours ago my hotel room brimmed with life. Fit for four, it now contains one man and his luggage, all awaiting the next thing.

September 17: Travel to Istanbul

I awoke at 8.30 a.m., mildly enthused by the idea of travel.

After breakfast, a man.

A luggage van.

A wait.

Another man.

A bus.

We alighted at a tucked-away ground-floor office within Dublin Airport. It's a place for special people who fly privately. We were herded like beasts into a pair of rooms prepared for our sole use. We grazed on cookies and wine. After a short wait we plodded through the x-ray facility.

A woman whose shirt was too small for her stomach halted my progress. She pointed to a screen showing a scan of my hand luggage. 'Can you tell me what this is sir?'

'My Mark-three-commercial.'

She seemed annoyed. 'You can't take a pistol on board.'

'But it's a Webley.'

'I'm taking it off you.'

'Yeah right — next you're going to tell me I can't smoke on the plane.'

She sat me down and explained it wasn't a private plane, it was a charter. There's a difference. A private flight is on a plane you own. We're hiring this one:

They thought we were Lynyrd Skynyrd

It's an Airbus A320; it can seat 180 passengers.

There are 34 of us.

For four hours it was a smooth and featureless flight, except for the novelty of being above the clouds for a change.

Approaching the airstrip in Istanbul, the details of the landscape were revealed: nothing says warm weather like a peppering of pastel-coloured buildings in brown fields.

We landed on the Asian side of Istanbul and stepped onto the tarmac amid dense, humid air. We got into one of those buses you only see at airports. The doors closed.

'Where's Charley?' came a voice.

We noticed Charley Webb still making her way down the plane steps.

Our bus pulled away.

Like a scene from a disaster movie, when someone pounds the glass of a soundproof lab and no one hears, we erupted into a chaos of yammering, trying to alert our driver he was leaving someone behind.

I fell to my knees clutching tissues, pleading with God.

Charley got into a spare van.

Eleven seconds later we reached the terminal building. We could've walked the hundred yards.

We strolled inside and handed our passports to a man with a hat.

A polite lady motioned us to wait in a room containing sofas, a TV, fridge full of booze, and trays of sweet baked goods.

I tried a sage tea and was instantly hooked.

I stuffed a decorative wooden box of teabags into my shirt.

The polite woman gave me a quizzical look.

'What are you gonna do, deport me?'

He face remained a tan sculpture.

'Fine,' I said, and replaced the box. I made sure to clamp a fistful of tea bags into my pocket, staring her out.

Going by the receipt in my passport it seems sixty dollars fills the criteria for entry into Turkey.

We get on another bus.

Dusk is becoming dark. On rolling hills, variously purposed buildings become silhouettes. Ahead, a river of brake lights snakes its way into the horizon.

The last time we visited Istanbul we stayed on the European side of the Bosphorus, in a vibrant area. Today it's an Asia-side hotel which can't decide on posh or building site. Shops in the base of the building stand dark.

Nine floors below my room is an outdoor swimming pool. In the immediate world beyond, squat purposeful buildings separate suburban arteries ferrying a constant stream of red and white lights in opposing directions.

Someone out there is hammering something metal.

There's a call to prayer floating on the breeze.

Occasional sirens.

In the distance dark high-rises come to life in twinkles of incandescence. Between there and here, green and red neon says something is happening. I'm not going out there, I'm knackered.

September 18: Istanbul, Day Off

I wrote to Elaine this morning:

MY SALT-AND-PEPPER FACE SITS ATOP A T-SHIRT TOO BIG FOR MY BODY, WHILE JAMMIE SHORTS COVER THE ONLY DIGNITY REMAINING. THROUGH THE WINDOW I SEE THE SCARBOROUGH OF WESTERN ASIA: GREY, TAN, AND UNINVITING.

I'm talking about Scarborough Ontario. It's a suburb of Toronto, a kind of concrete and tarmac jungle.

Through my window in Istanbul I see rivers of traffic. Near the base of the hotel, a perfectly square hole in the ground, soon to be a purposeful building; probably the origin of the sporadic hammering.

It even smells and sounds like Scarborough out there. Nothing particularly distasteful, just the whiff of petrol and some tarmacky *je ne sais quoi*. The swirling whine of tyres on hot road reminds me of my grandparents' house near the 401 Expressway.

According to an internet search the nearest Indian restaurant is 11 kilometres away — in Europe. Thankfully the hotel is adequate for short-term sanity.

I shan't be leaving here today.

Sometimes when visiting new places there's some anxiety, but it's not that. It's more logical; nothing I see jumps out at me. I'll be satisfied if I get to the pool and find something to eat in the hotel restaurant.

I didn't visit the pool but I got hungry. While waiting for an elevator to take me to food I looked out a window and saw another swimming pool with nobody in it, a small outdoor stage, a rusty electrical substation, cranes, and hi-rise buildings. No people.

I enjoyed a shandy and veggie wrap at the hotel bar.

Mickey came in and confirmed my suspicions: there's nothing around here.

September 19: Istanbul, Show Day

We have to do actual work today. A bit of general usefulness will do me some good after two days of looking out the window.

At breakfast Chris sports his 'Rolex' watch, a bargain he picked up yesterday on his adventures. It picks up only a minute every few hours.

Unlike the previous pair of grey days the morning is bright.

Man.

Van.

10 minutes of surprisingly light traffic.

Ülker Sports Arena, a new facility. It's a squat cylinder.

LOGISTICS

We scaled our equipment down for this gig. We had to air-freight the gear. The trucks wouldn't have made it from Dublin in time, although the drivers wanted to try. Air-freighting is expensive, and this stuff has to fly onward to Bucharest, then Verona. The Winning Team's rolling workstations have been replaced by small cases containing the bare minimum.

The only technical difficulty I faced during set-up was a rattle from Mitch's amp, set off by low frequency notes. A screwdriver took care of it. The output transformer had shaken a bit loose.

In the evening during a backstage wander something outside struck me. A waxing crescent moon of dull orange through a muslin haze. *How Turkish* I thought.

SHOWTIME

The show was delayed by 15 minutes because seats weren't filling fast enough.

With only minutes to go, Roscoe's bass rig developed an unsavoury noise. Chris and the audio guys found a problem within the amp's effects loop. The offending item was removed and the rig was saved with seconds to spare.

Istanbul's audience aren't the most vocal but they clap in time enthusiastically and often. There isn't much of a barrier separating stage and audience, and as we approach the encores they begin advancing on the stage. The standing crowd are inches from Leonard as *First We Take Manhattan* launches to thunderous claps which threaten to drown out the P.A.

Load-out is a bit frustrating. The local stagehands are woefully unskilled and the language barrier is a stone wall.

Many of them speak neither English nor Turkish; their native tongue is Kurdish. The few Turkish guys who can understand English can't speak Kurdish.

The local crew chief has almost no experience in this work, so getting anything done by proxy is nearly impossible.

Instructing the stagehands is mostly pointless. It takes longer to explain than it does to do it ourselves.

Some roadies get bent out of shape when this kind of thing happens but there's nothing you can do other than get on with it. In the end it only took around an hour to load the four small trucks.

We all pitched in and got it done.

1.38 a.m. With beers in hand we rode a small and crammed bus to the hotel.

2.02 a.m. Shower and a fix of internet.

2.21 a.m. I paid my incidentals and joined a few others who commandeered the hotel bar. It was shut but we brought our own booze. The place became a din of chatter and booze, and the only thing missing were the snacks.

No load-out food from the caterers tonight, but the promoters offered an alternative. Through another language barrier, instead of 18 sandwiches we got 18 pizzas. Even a cheeseless model for me.

3.06 a.m. A man and woman show up and sit at the bar.

Sloppy lips writhed, hands went wandering.

They eventually took it upstairs.

Before they vanished the woman spun and smiled at us. In her local accent she spoke in English: *time for sex!*

Right then, on you go.

4 a.m. A clear Russian Mistress unfurls invisible hair from beneath a golden cap. The vodka is surely sent by Dupuis. I whiff out the faintest tobacco hint. A dark figure approaches.

I got out of there.

I set my alarm for 6.10 a.m., brushed my teeth, zipped my luggage, and lay on the bed in my clothes.

I fear the scoundrel will rap my door as I drift away in a dark haze.

September 20: Travel to Bucharest

At a bleary-eyed 6.15, there's nothing to do but preen half-heartedly in the mirror to ensure I don't look like Hallowe'en. *Spectacles, testicles, wallet and watch*, out the door.

Looking out the window by the elevator, the navy sky is only just accepting a revitalising hint of orange. Jon and Dave are in the lobby already; Saint Paul is outside 'aving a fag.

6.32 a.m. Only a couple of minutes late, our crack squad of twelve are seated in two vans heading to Atatürk Airport in Europe. Our flight departs at 10.40, and the airport is only 40 minutes away if you trust the internet. Local knowledge says don't trust the internet.

Traffic in Istanbul is entertaining. There are few road markings and our driver steers like he's spinning a Catherine wheel. For the first time in days we get to see neighbourhoods with character. Minarets tipped in silvery crescents slice at a peach sky. Through the haze of a hundred miles, white clouds look like mountain ranges.

Chris's hundred-euro 'Rolex' piece of shit fell apart as he donned it this morning. He laughed about it. I think he liked the experience of the purchase and sees the watch as a keepsake of the moment: haggling with some dude behind a fake moustache over a knock-off clock that can't keep time.

'I'm an honest guy,' said the dealer.

Ahead, the Bosphorus, the strait dividing Asia and Europe. Halfway across the First Bosphorus Bridge* I look back to view the tree-lined banks of the Asian continent. An orange sun melts out of the leaves.

The bridge reminds me of the Golden Gate Bridge in California. As we reach the half-way point, a guy up front announces something none of us understand.

He probably felt like he was talking to a bunch of cats.

Through the unintelligible stream I thought I made out *Byzan*, but that's it.

Fact attack: Istanbul used to be Constantinople, which used to be Byzantium.

We arrived at the airport much earlier than our fears expected. It would be another hour until the check-in desk opened. We had teas and coffees, and once the desk was manned we spent an age in the queue. Each passenger checking in seemed to have a thousand questions.

'Is this the plane to Bucharest?'

'Yes.'

'What time does it leave?'

'Ten-forty.'

'How many wings does it have?'

'I'm going to hurt you.'

Next up, another queue; around 150 people at passport control.

Now; you and me — we wait in line.

SOME people simply choose a spot in the queue.

A pleasant looking young lady showed up. She wore a tattoo of arab-looking script. With the aid of a male partner she performed an amazing *Euro-barge*, cutting ahead 50 people.

Her male accomplice wore distressed blue jeans and carried a mobile phone wrapped in a piece of paper. He unhooked the velvet rope, she entered, and he re-clasped it. You have to appreciate the confidence. Such majesty. All the same... Must... Contain... Rage...

The plane took off and nothing happened.

Descending into Bucharest, the earth was a patchwork of brown fields dotted with cows. Wheels chirped on tarmac and we raced by two beat-up old planes put out to pasture.

We were met in the terminal by a pair of local promoter reps; they led us to a van for luggage, then another for us.

On the way to the hotel we pass monument after statue and statue after monument. On the final stretch we see the unmissable *People's House*, also known as the *House of the Republic* and the *Palace of Parliament*.

The building is fucking immense.

Locals say it's the second-largest building in the world, complete with fourteen underground floors, most of which are off limits to the public. There's talk of a tunnel linking the building directly with the airport.

I only had two hours' sleep last night. I have no desire to go out and explore. Apparently there's a rock bar in town. Not for me today, I preferred the hotel bar.

Others came and went, and Saint Paul and I stayed to the last.

* *Fact attack: an English barber in Larne told me he worked on the Bosphorus Bridge. Apparently they designed it while building it.*

September 21: Bucharest, Day Off

It's a grey drizzly morning. My room overlooks elevated grass courts, shrubs, and air vents. A mixed community of trees make a border between the hotel grounds and an endless sea of chalky, ten-storey buildings; the infinite distance is cut with prickles of antennae.

The hotel is modern and spacious, classy yet sparse. High-end shops line the ground floor corridors. You could buy a stately watch (Chris?) or some designer clothes.

We've been here before, in Septembers 2008 and 2009. Back then I strolled among stray dogs. The area around the hotel remains quite uninspiring. This time I notice fewer strays.

Expensive cars sparkle in the crescent driveway. At the centre of the arc stands a statue — an angel in flowing robes holding a trumpet in one hand and in her free arm, an incapacitated man.

I'm hooked.

I'm sober with nothing better to do. I embark on the biggest fact-attack yet.

The sculptor was Wladimir Hegel and the bronzed man appears to be Pavel Zăgănescu. In 1848, when Romania was (technically) Wallachia, Zăgănescu led a division of firemen into battle against Ottoman troops. The bronze Zăgănescu clutches a small eagle standard to his chest. His jacket is topped with epaulettes and at his feet sits his plumed fireman's helm.

If you stand behind the statue you can see a little cannon barrel under Zăgănescu's foot. On Wikipedia I found a depiction of the battle; cannon are plainly visible, as are the firemen's helms and fezzes of the Ottoman soldiers.

The battle took place on Spirii Hill, which the angel now faces. For centuries power has lived up there. Churches, princely residences and palaces have stood on its crest, each making way for the next symbol of power. Like Wembley's Harrow on the Hill, you have to wonder how far back its significance stretches.

That giant building I mentioned yesterday — it stands up there as a testimony of one man's lengthy stay of power and his rapid downfall.

The Romanian Revolution of 1989 claimed the lives of dictator Nicolae Ceaușescu and his wife Elena. They fled the building in fear but were captured. They were quickly tried, convicted, and sentenced to death. Machine gun fire took care of it.

What's interesting for me is how the statue outside the hotel is twined with the big house.

Zăgănescu and his angel stood on that hill in 1901.

In 1984 they were uprooted to make way for Ceaușescu's massive house.

Exactly five and a half years after construction began, the Ceaușescus were executed.

Less than nine months later, and exactly 99 years after its inauguration, the Firefighter's Monument was hauled to its feet once more.

Now it looks onto the hill, to the giant house.

Power lives on that hill. An angel was evicted and now she faces it as if to say you can build whatever you like, but divine power is untouchable. I like to think she holds her trumpet in warning — if you're a dick, God will fuck you up.

Imagine if the Ceaușescus' fates were sealed the moment they toppled the statue. To build on the hill is to meddle with power. Nicolae messed not only with Zăgănescu and his angel, but the people of Romania. If only he'd listened to Spiderman's uncle Ben: *with great power comes great responsibility*.

The Ceaușescus were executed December 25, Gregorian Christmas, 1989.

On January 7, 1990, Christmas Day for many of the Orthodox faith, the death penalty in Romania was abolished. Two Christmases; the death of darkness and the birth of forgiveness.

Toot toot — God's gonna be pissed

DO TIMES EVER CHANGE?

At this hotel, new money changes hands for both legitimate and illicit purposes. Prostitutes are busy at night, aided by a man or two setting up transactions in and around the lobby. Last night outside the hotel (admittedly I was a little tipsy) I spoke with a ~~pimp~~ taxi driver named — not making this up — Romeo. He was chatty with the girls, supplying names of guests they would call on. But he's a taxi driver, honestly, his car is in the parking lot.

Anyway Romeo, in his early thirties, spoke fondly of the communist days. He told me everyone had jobs. He seemed to reserve a special place in his thoughts for Gorbachev.

'Gorbachev?' I said.

He corrected my pronunciation stressing the difference; 'Gorba*chuv*.' (The *u* sounded like an *oo*.)

My childhood memories are laced with memories of Reagan, Andropov, *Gorbachuv*, and how America seemed to despise the Soviets. On my TV, communism was synonymous with despair and personal restrictions. Here one enterprising young man seems to revere it.

September 22: Bucharest, Show Day

The Winning Team waits outside the hotel. It's a nice day.

Man and van are late.

We're told the venue is only five minutes away. Walking would require effort. Admittedly it's about time I did something useful. Work might clear my head of the infatuation I have for that big feckin' house.

Man and van arrive. They take us somewhere.

The venue is an outdoor stage in an open space facing — guess what? That bloody building. Its innumerable windows are like eyes watching everything. When you look at it from the hotel you're a comfortable voyeur; the monstrous edifice seems unbothered. Here at the end of *Bulevardul Uniri* there's no safety from the sentient glare of the People's House. Behind the stage, the spacious boulevard is divided by fountains and shrubs stretching into the distance. Expensive cars bark, their throttles opened by boy racers keen on reaction.

Around 3 p.m., Mickey points out that the boulevard has been closed down, fenced off. A stationary fire truck straddles the lanes. An officer of the bomb squad appears and introduces himself to me, asking if we've seen anything or anyone suspicious. Having grown up in Northern Ireland, the meeting feels somewhat nostalgic.

45 minutes before the show a murder of squawking black feathers flew over the stage. Hundreds of crows congregate on the stepped palace hill. Are these the eyes of the building at night?

The tickets said the show would start at 8.30 p.m.

Curfew is supposed to be 11; it would make for a short gig.

Curfew extended.

The band took the stage.

Fact attack: this is our first show to start in the dark.

The audience are polite and quiet; so quiet I can hear one woman's bangles rattling through the applause. The temperature is agreeable and the air is quite still. With no reflective surfaces the acoustics are what you might call dead. Ordinarily slap-back can be a problem for sound engineers, but a tiny bit doesn't hurt. The crows' feathers are probably soaking up the sound.

Like I said earlier it was a nice day. And I'm sober; this means I get contemplative. Humour me.

I'm still thinking of communism, wondering what it must have been like growing up here. The audience seem so reserved; did the Soviet model instil in people a notion that enjoyment was a distraction from workful purpose? Today's Bucharest is abundant with the signs of material excess — flash clothes, fast cars and fit women for rent. But this audience are so well-behaved, almost regimented.

They start to warm up. In the quiet, crystal-white tractor beam of a spotlight, Leonard dons a pair of prescription sunglasses; 'Forgive this rock 'n roll affectation, but I can't see a damn thing.'

A few chuckles.

Later in the set Leonard introduces each band member. The most enthusiastic cheer frightened away the crows when he introduced Alex, native of Moldova, Romania's friendly neighbour.

Nearing the end, the People left their seats to be closer to the man they came to see. They sing in whispers, but their numbers roar; 19,000 ecstatic faces get a taste of a few more songs, their backs turned to the all-seeing building.

Lit by a legion of sodium lamps, the People's House bears witness to *oamenii obisnuiti** and their innocent moments of excess. Leonard keeps them out past the original curfew, taking them right to the wire, to a time fixed by the last trains.

* Many thanks to Emilia Serban (via Twitter) for the direction on the usage of oamenii obisnuiti, *Romanian for* 'everyday people'.

September 23: Travel to Verona

Lufthansa.

Bucharest to Munich.

Munich to Verona.

We got to the hotel around 5.30 p.m.

This is the home of Shakespeare's Romeo and Juliet. I studied that play once. Never seen it live. According to touristy publications, Juliette's house is just off *Via Capello*. The fictional character has been immortalised in bronze and supposedly it's good luck to rub her breast.

I approached a man so fat he needed two mobility scooters to get around. His moustache looked like dyed kitchen roll. One foot was terribly swollen, the other a nub. Flies buzzed around him.

'Excuse me is this Via Capello?'

'Si señor.'

'What the fuck country am I in?'

'No habla Ingles.'

'Look, how much to rub the girl's tit?'

'Thirty euro señor.'

'Does God know you tell lies?'

'Si.'

I handed over the money and he snatched at it. He pointed to a balcony and there she was.

I climbed a dank stairwell and found an open door, splintered and patched. The room was mouldy. Floor boards squealed under my weight and I emerged onto a rickety balcony. I examined the statue.

'Wait a minute!'

It wasn't Juliette, it was Katerina. Petruchio married her for a bet.

The fat liar sped off on his synchronised scooters with my money, guffawing. All I had was a bronzed Katerina staring at me.

I muttered to myself. 'Well you paid your money you might as well grab a handful of the shrew's boob.'

I reached out.

She blinked.

Living statue scared the fuck out of me, I nearly shit myself.
She cackled like a crone.
I panicked and punched her in the face.

My police cell smelt like piss. Mike bailed me out and gave me a stern talking-to.

My hotel room has a small cove of a window and I can't see much from it. An orange sky gathers, clouds reflecting street lamps. The air is thick and humid — I smell rain. Juliette, Juliette, where's your rack at?

September 24: Verona Show

Today is Elaine's birthday and I'd prefer to be home. Two weeks to go.
We're back on the bus.
Kristoff drives us to the venue.
The venue and/or promoter didn't want our trucks to unload until 11 a.m., three hours after the ideal. Last night's production hadn't finished loading out and they needed this morning to complete the process. Questioning the pace of work in Italy is pointless; it usually leads to further delay. Italian crews work at Italian paces and today is an Italian day. You just have to obey their *Law of Not Giving a Shit.* It's no wonder Rome wasn't built in a day.
In the narrow street, the mood among the local crew is jovial as they unload heavy audio cases amid stone buildings. Tall and narrow windows are protected by shutters fixed with rusty hinges.
The venue is a Roman amphitheatre dating back to around AD 30; the pink and white limestone façade has been worn down through the millennia. Its base sits five feet below modern street level.
Down the street is a piazza bound by four-storey buildings fronted with colonnades, capitaled in leafy motifs, topped by square, pyramidal roofs clad with clay tiles.
There's bugger all to do until the backline truck gets unloaded. I spy a little shop; it's time for crisps. Potato chips. Whatever.
I couldn't wait; my excitement gathered on the approach. This is going to be good. Ordered rows of colour-coded salty snacks will dazzle me; I'll be spoilt, driven to distraction, unable to choose between plush spuds of variety, thinly sliced, deep-fried to gold.
I enter, rubbing my hands together.

It was a dark hole crowded with postcards, trinkets and fucking Haribo.

No crisps.

Cunts.

Crestfallen, with time to kill, I stroll around the arena. There are 72 entrances, each assigned a numeral. Roman, as it happens. The trucks are unloading at 36; I have little better to do than seek number one; or *I* if you prefer. Surely it'll be worth looking at.

Street performers are everywhere, but there's one I can't take my eyes off. His body is hidden behind a baby's pram, and a blanket hides his bulk. His head pokes into the seating compartment and a headless doll is strapped to his chin. He's a big-headed baby in a pram. His schtick: squeaking an awful high-pitched kazoo-type whistly thing, responding dynamically to his audience's attention. I can't understand why no one, absolutely nobody, is stoning him to death.

I found gate *I*.

Meh.

Back to the trucks. Maybe I'm needed.

Around gate LX, I found something I overlooked earlier. It looked like the main entrance to the amphitheater, almost like a tall foyer. It followed the venue's radius, it was crumbly and hang on a minute, this isn't an add-on…

It turns out an earthquake shook the amphitheatre in 1117, bringing down most of the outer ring; this was its remains. Latin is chiseled in the stone; you don't see that at gate 36.

Yay me, I'm an intrepid explorer with no friggin' crisps.

Attached to this broken outer ring, way at the top, is an array of stadium lighting. The metalwork is strapped in place. It looks about as safe as Dad using a cigarette lighter to look into the car engine. That's Italy.

As a concert venue, about the only good thing about this ancient site is the steel plating over the cobbles. At least we can get the cases on stage without clumsily rolling them over a bone-shaking floor.

The inside of gate 36 is an arched, time-blackened tunnel. I imagine countless individuals entering this portal: revered performers, gladiators, poor bastards thrown to the beasts. I think Death might have liked this place. Emerging from the tunnel you see the real amphitheatre, or what remains of it. The original floor is entirely covered by stage, orchestra pit, and modern seating. Around half the space is allotted to the audiences; beside and behind the stage, the other half is off-limits.

Directly opposite is gate I; it doesn't seem to stand out much from 36. However above it, there's a little section of seating surrounded by a balustrade. You wonder who might have sat in such a spot and what their fates were.

The steps leading there are a modern aluminium, with painted treads of red and handrail of gold. All the best seats in the house are red, with gold seats coming second, and the rest, stone-cold tiers of the original structure. The seats in what I'm calling the royal box are black. This evening's royal family will be spotlight operators, the tools of their trade lying disassembled.

We are delayed. The P.A. is taking forever to get up and running because of a ~~lie~~ miscommunication. An agreement was made ages ago: we'd use the venue's sound system, but the speakers aren't where they're supposed to be.

The physical placement of the speakers determines where Leonard stands on stage. Imagine yourself floating above the stage. Your head points to the audience, your feet backstage. P.A. speakers flank the stage. Draw an imaginary line linking them. Leonard has to stand behind this line or else we risk crazy feedback. If the speakers are far away from the audience, Leonard is further away still. In Verona he's miles away. Don't blame us, we think of this stuff weeks, sometimes months in advance.

That's Italy.

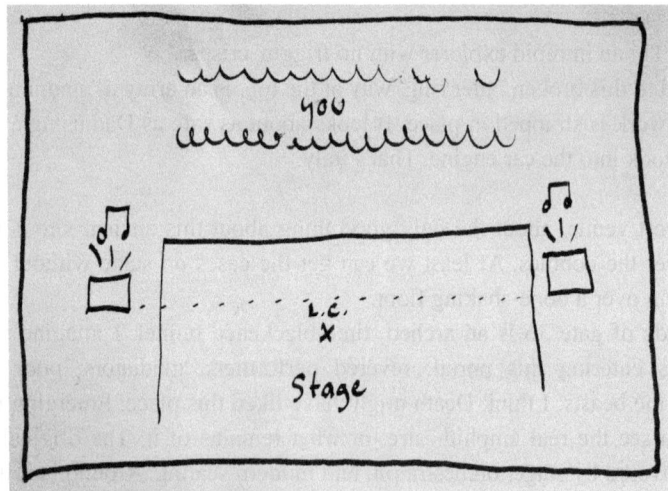

The day drags on. Eventually the Winning Team are up. We laid carpets, set up and checked the backline.

Weather says rain.

We covered up.

A passing shower, nothing we can't handle.

We uncovered.

With a cheeky grin Mickey goads the sky; 'Is that the best you can do?'

I wince. 'Umm, Mickey?'

'Yeah?'

'Do you have any idea how many gods have been angered in this place?'

'What about them.'

'You don't think some of them might be looking a little payback?'

Verona is our last outdoor show of the year. After tonight it'll be indoors all the way to December in North America. We just need to hang on for one more.

4 p.m.

Mickey has angered the gods.

Neptune, god of water-things. Jupiter, god of sky and thunder. They shook hands and took revenge. The worst rain in my 17 years of outdoor festivals. Everything got wet. At once. The stage has a roof but it's so tall it affords little cover from driven rain. We're outflanked and the plastic sheeting was undone by wind. We scrambled to cover anything we could with whatever we could and had no choice but to ride the storm out, hoping for the best under wind, water, thunder and lightning.

The wind settled but the rain kept coming. With the gear secured against a watery grave, we noticed the front of the stage was a pool. Standing water had one place to go, wicking into the carpets — our precious carpets! We squeegeed what we could off the stage, but the worst was done.

We looked like we'd been in a hurricane. Dishevelled and soaked, the sun finally came out. The gods grew tired of us and moved on.

Cleanup began; fortunately nothing was damaged and soundcheck went ahead, albeit late. By this point I'd been on my feet much of the day and I was getting crazy hungry. I shovelled dinner into my face and got ready for the show.

The stars were out; no clouds meant no rain. We did away with the set drapes in case of wind, but otherwise it was a normal show. It started at 9 p.m., and ran until 12.30 a.m.

The Winning Team watched the truck doors close around 2 a.m.

None of this would've happened if I had rubbed Juliette's ju-jubes.

Verona

September 25: Travel to Toulon

I awoke in the bus and reminded myself we made it out of Verona unscathed. My shoes had only dried a few hours ago. Now it's a bright new day and we're on our way to Toulon. We thread through Alpine tunnels, along high roads, soaring above knots of sun-soaked houses, their roofs clad in earthy red tiles.

My hotel room is small but adequate; around a hundred square feet. A patio door leads to a parallelogram balcony.

The outdoor pool is surrounded by palm trees. A dual carriageway is divided by palm and grass, and in the near distance rolling hills are warm and lush.

My room has a bed, desk, and a thing to put a TV in. There's a coffee maker but it frightens me.

There's a little mall nearby.

I found a health food shop.

A pair of identical twins worked there. One male, one female. They had bowl haircuts and wore overalls. I hated them instantly.

98

'Hey, you got any tofu wieners?'

The guy only spoke French but his sister understood. Her accent was weird; she was like Megatron with auto-tune. 'Yes monsieur.'

'How much?'

'Three euros.' God, she's like the voice of Nintendo.

They had tomato juice too. 'Can I get a bulk discount?'

'Pardon monsieur?' She had gappy teeth.

I rolled my eyes and engaged the universal translator: 'DISCOUNT?!'

'How many do you want to buy?'

'One.'

I went to my room and ate tofu dogs with mustard.

The internet sucks here. *Shitternet*.

Around 7 p.m., I couldn't keep my eyes open but managed a phone conversation with Elaine.

'I'm sorry I missed your birthday, baby.'

'Was it fun?'

'Fuck no. Soaked to the skin.'

'You looking forward to getting home?'

'Is the pope a brownshirt?'

'Love you.'

'Love you too.'

I perked up and wanted beer. I joined a few doomed UHTC souls at the hotel bar. It was lively like an embalming ritual. After a pair of forced beers I couldn't hack it any longer and went to bed.

September 26: Toulon, Show Day

Those bloody carpets. They were dripping wet when they rolled into the truck after Verona. SOME of the Winning Team left the hotel this morning to go in and deal with them. Other members of the Winning Team felt no obligation to do so.

In a barren driveway behind the venue, Chris, Dan and I hung the heavy, sodden rugs over a fence. It was a continuous grid of enamelled steel crested with sharp points. You claw at the grid with one hand and pull yourself up onto the fence footing — concrete road dividers — and hang the black and smelly, 264 square feet of dripping grossness over your head and along the fence.

We should be at least grateful for the space and conditions; it's dry and partly sunny.

The process for the reds was similar but they're thicker, weighed down with more water. It took three of us to lift each damnable thing. A man at each end pulling himself up with the roll, a man in the middle supporting.

Lift, unfurl, lift unfurl.

Do it twice more.

Tear your flesh on the sharp points if you want.

Thankfully only three of the five rugs were soaked. A bit of an allegory; only three of the five of us turned up to do it.

Unload the gear, look it over in the spacious area behind the stage.

We're indoors for the rest of the year. No more solar blankets and plastic sheeting; no more wind and shaky stages. No more rain. From now until Christmas it's stale, grimly-lit venues.

It was time for the Winning Team to sprinkle the magic beans. The black rugs were still damp, they'll stay outside.

The reds are integral to the show.

They're squelchy and smell gross.

There was plenty to do today but at least there was no weather to fuck things up. It's surprising how much extra work the elements add.

A casualty. The fingerboard of Roscoe's upright bass is dislodged from the neck.

Inoperable.

This kind of repair needs a man with a beard and a fixed address. Fortunately we have a backup. It's a skinny electric fretless and it looks... Different. Oh, and it's in rough shape — it sounds crackly.

Boffin time.

I thought it best to extricate a suspect potentiometer* and create a static electrical equivalent on the circuit board.

And then the battery clip wore out. I replaced it.

Then it gets silly. The bass sounds fine through a test amp in Guitar World,** but out on stage it sounds like it's dying.

Fuck it, put it back in its case and let's never speak of it again.

The emergency surgery means a hasty dinner. I inhaled a bagel and soup.

It's a 'compressed day'. Everything gets done but there's little time to think.

When Leonard takes the stage he speaks in French, telling the audience the usual deal: 'Tonight we're going to give you everything we got.' That's what I assume he's saying. I speak and understand a little French, but here in Guitar World we can barely hear what he's saying. We're behind the speakers and it's a different world of sound. For all we know he's telling the crowd he's gonna play Kiss songs all night.

But in Monitor World they can hear him, so if there's anything really crazy going on we'll know about it eventually.

At the end of the first set Leonard skips off stage and the audience go mental. Something's not right. As usual the band remain on stage playing Leonard off, but there's never this much applause at this point.

Leonard usually tells the audience the show will break and come back.

He didn't tonight. The crowd thinks this is the end and they're hooting for encores. A man appears on stage, speaks French, and the audience laughs at themselves.

It took a record-setting 46 minutes for the Winning Team to get their crap into the truck. My feet are tired and sore. I need a drink.

A potentiometer is the electrical thing connected to the knob you twirl when altering the volume of your hi-fi, guitar, or ancient TV set.

**Guitar World is a little nest in the stage left wing where Mickey and I call home, carrying out repairs and keeping instruments safe.*

September 27: Travel to Paris

In my bunk I'm awoken by the intensity of a full bladder. There's a little window in here and daylight floods a pair of bloodshot eyes. We've stopped in a service area on the way to Paris. I'm sore and stiff and I hobble into the cramped loo. While I'm poised over the tiny toilet the bus pulls away with a series of judders and I'm jostled in a 3 x 4 room with my pants falling around my ankles.

Someone bangs on the door. 'Who the fuck's in there?'

'Someone's in here!'

'I know, who the fuck?' The bus hits a bump and I leave my feet.

'It's me!' A sharp corner. I slip on spots of urine and bang my head on the sink. 'Gah!'

'You better not be shitting in there!'

'I'm not shitting!' The bus lurches and I'm thrown against the door.

'It sounds like you're shitting!'

I fall out the loo, bare ass to the sky. Nobody there. I gotta go back to bed, I'm out of my mind.

Some two hours later we arrived in Paris. The traffic sucked; it always does here. This was the last drive of the leg and it's planes from now on. Kristoff drives away, joining the escargot-like traffic.

I dragged my luggage through the hotel corridors and found my room. It was tall, bright and rectangular, wide as I entered. It said *calm*.

I phoned downstairs.

'Bonjour, je le something or other, what do you want in French?'

'Hey is that reception?'

'Yes sir.'

'This room is fucking awesome! I love the dominant colour scheme of red, black, and grey-brown. The desk is modern, stained black, and the glass top is clutter-free. No one does that!'

'I'm — glad you like it monsieur.'

'Fuckin' *A* I like it. And that art-deco print you got going on. How did you know I loved deco?'

'Um, monsieur—'

'Shut up and two beds, that is so cool! Which one should I sleep in?'

'I am hanging up now monsieur.'

'Fuck it ok thanks dude.'

As soon as I tried connecting to the internet I regretted telling Pepe how much I loved the room. Daylight robbery for 512K shitternet.

It started to rain out.

After the rain I went for a bite. The avenue is lined with trees. A bold, near-full moon is on the rise against a pale backdrop of waning daylight. The air is comfortable but autumn is on the way. The streets are jammed with every petrol-quaffing vehicle you can think of, and the smell of two-stroke engines follow moped riders in grey-blue puffs.

I strolled around the block. Four right-angles and on each side of this square was a half-dozen folks with their hands out. Everywhere, thin and curvy neon scripts advertise. The pavement becomes a metal grid; it breathes gusts of warm air. The metro is an underground dragon threading Parisians through webs of tunnels below the congestion of surface dwellers.

They eat so much meat here it's crazy. Vegetarians must be few and far between. I find an Italian joint near the hotel. It's kinda pedestrian, but whatever.

The waiter came. He was shiny bald, and he had a moustache. Beats me why.

I ordered my food in French. 'Une bureau cn gros et une bowl of paskeddi see-voo-play.'

He puffed his lips.

'What.'

He went off to get my food.

There's a woman sitting near me; she's talking on the phone while eating. I think she's Dutch. Her words are a waterfall of grunts.

The waiter came with my beer.

I forgot to bring a book with me so I amuse myself. I tap the table with my fork. '*Cellllll-afuckin-brate-good-times-come-on-ah! Woooo!*'

Chatty-food-face isn't pleased with me one bit. She gives me the evil eye.

'*There's a party goin' on right here-ah! A celebration-ah! To last throughout the year-ah!*'

She's wearing a turtleneck sweater. She talks louder into her phone.

The party can't be ignored. '*SO BRING YO' GOOD TIMES-AH! AND YO LAUGHTER TOO-AH! WE GON' CELEBRATE AN—*'

She throws her phone at me. 'SHUT UP SHUT UP SHUT UP SHUT UP!'

I dodge her shitty Nokia. It smacks against the window. I pout. The guy comes with my food. The woman is breathing heavy, she's probably out of shape.

The battery won't go back on her phone.

I twirl some noodles on my fork and mumble falsetto '*It's time — to come together...*'

September 28: Paris Show 1

The Winning Team arrived at L'Olympia in time to find a cramped stage. The capacity is 1,952, the smallest venue of our European leg. Despite the lack of cat-juggling space on stage it's a pleasant environment. The local crew are helpful, the place is clean, and the backstage area is comfortable.

The audience will sit in folding seats of red fabric with little wooden armrests. There's a mezzanine, its balcony a crescent.

You'll recall Roscoe's bass, the unglued fingerboard. Chris took it to 'a guy on the other side of Paris.' He re-glued the fingerboard, repaired a couple of splits, and refitted the internal sound post. It's common after such a repair that an instrument may need a tweak.

SOUNDCHECK

As usual Leonard soundchecks, just him and a guitar. You can hear the clichéd pin drop. During *The Singer Must Die*, Roscoe and Chris were slightly off stage, inspecting the newly repaired bass.

Bam!

Clunk!

Sprunk!

P'toing!

They're pounding on this bass with some tool I can't identify.

An image appears in my head. The scene in *This is Spinal Tap*, where bassist Derek Smalls is trapped in a set piece, some sort of pod. A roadie comes out with a hammer and bangs on the pod during a quiet bit of the song. That's kinda what's happening now. From an audience perspective in the soft seats I'm incredulous.

Backline techs are mostly concerned with footprints; we tend to think in two dimensions, forgetting about height. Out here I get the full picture of a Leonard Cohen show. The tall and expansive drapes are brilliant with strong light. Alone on stage, Leonard is dwarfed by a shimmering vertical sea. It isn't flashy or avant-garde, it's a big sky above a guy with a guitar.

The rest of the band are apparently stuck in traffic and the full soundcheck is delayed, but it happens without much drama.

SHOWTIME

Here in Guitar World behind the veils of sheer deceit*, you're in a bit of a sensory deprivation realm. I can't really see the audience, nor can I hear much. The acoustics are pretty dead. But when *The Partisan* rolls around, you know the audience are out there. They cheer through the verses, and at the end stamp and applaud. The tall and narrow drapes flanking the main backdrop are soaked in a deep red reminiscent of France's darker times.

The crowd are on their feet for the encores. There's no barrier and if they wanted they could get on stage and grab a handful of damp and smelly carpet.

Peeking through the veils I see audience faces are none-more-bright; after *It if Be Your Will*, Leonard calls for *Save the Last Dance*.

He goes off.

He comes back.

I Tried to Leave You.

The cushy red seats are snapped closed, the entire crowd upright and hollering.

No load-out. It's a quick job to switch everything off, get the guitars into their cases and leave our walkie-talkies into the production office to be recharged. Beers and sandwiches await us backstage.

Man.

Van.

Room.

September 29: Paris Show 2

I sat at my desk enjoying a cup of tea. The water was heated by one of those monsteriffic coffee makers. It spews clean hot water, not a whiff of ancient coffee like you get with the 80s machines still found in some hotels.

I'm going in early today.

In the lobby I await a man and his van.

It's a bright morning. The hotel sits on a narrow street near a busy junction. Right across from us is a building site. It looks like they're upgrading a public square. Beyond that is a long terrace of buildings, a continuing apex of slate roofs, chimneys, dormers, and windows. There are tiny balconies; hanging from cast iron rails are flower boxes exploding with striking red petals. People walking past the hotel are dressed in a range of seasons. Some cling to summer while others prefer autumn.

Man and van.

Traffic.

Above the theatre entrance is a marquee. Like most it has modular characters to shuffle and replace, but these are vermilion neon. My mind is a little bit blown; somewhere in L'Olympia there's a room full of electric letters.

I'm early for a few reasons. I need to measure voltages and observe bias points of the 6V6 valves in Mitch's main Fender Supersonic. I also want free internet. Lastly I hope to collect the laundry I sent out yesterday.

SHOWTIME

We think Leonard's going to call a bunch of audibles tonight so we'd better be on our toes. We should be on our toes every night, but that would get in the way of cookin' up smack in Guitar World.

In the end the only deviation from the norm was *Different Sides* popping up at short notice in the encores.

At this point you'd do well to abandon any hope that something really amazing is going to happen during a show. Consistency is the key to good shows; when nothing really happens for us, we know we've done our jobs. Excitement speeds time up, but it can indicate problems.

AFTER THE SHOW

Dan and I did the streets of Paris for a few beers. We found a quiet strip club and hung out with the dancers. Paolo was from Brazil. His skin was like tanned chrome. Peanut was from Alabama, the token white guy with a baseball cap. They taught us some moves on the pole and I threw up on stage.

Around 3 a.m., I returned to my room.

There's a little fridge.

With barely a thought I opened the gateway to last-minute, desperately overpriced alcohol.

Presently I was stumped by the appearance of a curio: a calling card of heavy matte black paper. Along its edges I discerned a microscopic script. My eyes compressed under their lids as I struggled in vain to grasp the codex.

A faint whiff of tobacco emanated from the mysterious card. The processes of memory unraveled the archives and the tabooed name undarkened itself: Dupuis.

Mindless, the jittery crests of my fingerprints imprinted the cold dew of a beer can.

Rap rap rap at my door.

My fingers froze, the trance molested. A bead of sweat tumbled down my temple. I summoned a whisper and grimaced. 'Be gone.'

Rap rap rap.

My body tensed. 'Be gone I say!'

Rap rap rap.

My vision pinkened and I rose, driven away from the blackness of Dupuis' ingenious hypnosis. I tossed the scamp's calling card aside and it flickered away in a helix.

I prepared my salvo for the interloper, this late-night caller who would dare drive a wedge between a man and his deserving golden hops.

The refrigerator door closed of its own gravity.

I tore the door open and bellowed. 'I SAID BE G—'

The door swung wide and banged on the stopper.

Emptiness greeted me.

I craned my neck into the hallway; to the left a shrinking perspective of door frames. To the right an elevator landing bathed in halogen yellow. On the sandy tile floor, a shadow of feathered wings melted away.

I sped to the area dumbfounded. No one there.

Head shaking as I closed the door, muttering befuddlements of all kinds, I saw on my floor Dupuis' black invitation to insanity had become ashen. The hunger of bright flame devoured the remaining material and it wisped out in a tiny billow. I was saved. God knows how, but I was saved.

As I breathed silently under the covers, my restless eyes patrolled the blackness, remaining fearful until slumber took me.

Dupuis will attempt to strike again — he always does.

September 30: Paris Show 3

I have a small headache. It's a pittance to pay for the mysterious intervention that delivered me from Dupuis' invitation, the slick fuck.

It's Sunday.

The least I could hope for would be roast potatoes but this is France and the equivalent is probably boiled antler.

I came to work early for the internet. I skyped home to ensure everyone was alive and free from boils.

I unpacked the guitars, switched stuff on and made sure it served some sort of function.

Soundcheck today is unsurprisingly like yesterday; songs are rehearsed and snippets are sung. 11 bars of *Dance Me*, 12 of *The Future*. Mickey unveils a cardboard tube of identically pressed crisps. I promise him the world for just one saddle-shaped flatwork of reconstituted potato.

From a technical standpoint the show was... mostly uninteresting. It's the third show in the same venue. Everything blends.

Nope, nothing else going on.

Alright I can't lie. There was a goof.

One of Mitch's guitars does double duty. You have to give it different tunings for two different songs. There's a capo involved.

I handed him the guitar perfectly in tune... for the wrong song.

Twernnng.

He gave me a quick sidelong glance and I cradled my head in disbelief. He snapped on the tuner pedal and tuned while I wrote a suicide note.

Shit happens.

I wish it didn't but sometimes you make a mistake. When you do backline you take the show on board. If you fuck it up, well... Occasionally you make a superb landing in the wrong airport.

Next is the friggin' environment.

Normally it's fine to leave a guitar out on stage for 15 minutes before it's played but tonight the temperature spiked. Two nylon-string guitars fell victim and some of their strings sharpened in pitch. I spent the rest of the night criticising each string pluck, tuning and tuning again. Each passing minute without disaster was a relief.

The Winning Team ends a Parisian residency with a little dance. Leonard invited us on stage for a final shindig. I tore off my shirt and fell into the audience.

October 2012

October 1: Travel to Barcelona

I'm bummed I didn't get out and see more of Paris. I've been here several times but I don't recall many moments of fine appreciation. I remember once visiting the Eiffel Tower drunk.

We fly out of Charles de Gaulle airport. It's huge and looks like *The Jetsons*. It's a snapshot of the 70s, a concrete fantasy world where tall skyways ferry traffic. At nearly 40 years old they still somehow look futuristic.

Terminal 2 is a vastness of space. We're like blood cells in a giant concrete vein. At gate F28 a ceiling of perforated metal sheets covers curved glass. It's like a hive, or maybe even the inside of a mechanical butterfly.

Air France take us to Barcelona

We land at El Prat (try not to laugh) airport. The space is wider and taller than CDG, with shiny, glass-like floors. It seems so quiet given the volume of people.

Man.

Bus.

Under a vast blue canopy we're hotel-bound. There's a grey-brown haze floating in the distant horizons.

Approaching Barcelona, palm tress dot the land and interesting buildings jump out. Hotel Porta Fira looks like a big red vase. A round pod atop the Hesperia Tower sits like a heavy fascinator. The building seems inspired by Stickle Bricks.

Ronda del Litoral is a tarmac vein separating shipyards and sea containers from hillside Montjuïc Cemetery, a tiered resting place cut into the hill.

Hotel.

'Watch out for thieves.'

Last time we visited the Hotel Arts Barcelona, two of our lot fell victim to invisible villains.

Tonight we party, toasting the end of the tour. (Only three gigs to go.) We'll have a booze-up in the hotel bar, courtesy of Leonard.

At 7 p.m., my party senses are tingling. I slick my eyebrows with spit and cop a cuff of whiffed breath. I close my door behind me, strut down the hallway whistling *It's a Long Way to Tipperary*. I enter the elevator and press a button.

Descending, a thought jumps out at me: *mojitos*.

It was all very civilised at first. Then the collective drunk gene kicked in and some of us predisposed to crazy ramped up the atmosphere. I think we hired the bar or a function room beside it, I don't know. It was just us, a UHTC beast in its lair.

The iPods and speakers came out.

Flock of Seagulls, the Mission, the Cure, probably the Clash, who knows, the music was free and so was the booze.

Amaretto — Paul's favourite toast. The drink flowed like mountain streams as we danced around a font of debauchery.

The sinister malcontent rises.

From beneath a shimmering pool of clear rum lilypadded with mint leaves, a dark figure violently breaks the surface. The white foam of his emergence tosses lime wedges in a roiling surf.

Rum drips from his hat. His eyes are like polished steel. He beckons me with his flaming finger.

Once I might have resisted this monstrous heathen, but on this night I am his easy prey, his slave, his fancy-boy with wide eyes and gaping mouth. He grasps a rectangular bottle and levels it. I skip and shimmy to the glittery red stream flowing from this bottomless vessel.

Into my chasm he pours.

I am a hooked fish spinning around the line. I twirl under the jet of almondy sweetness, my arms outstretched, feet tipee-toeing in a free jazz pirouette.

I am Dupuis' plaything.

The night could have spider-webbed into a million instances of degeneracy, of sin, of sybaritism, I cannot know for I am no longer in control.

The last thing I remember is removing my shirt and turning to my colleagues; it's like being in the spotlight. I face a stunned and silent gathering aghast at my doughy torso.

Dupuis invisibly gorges on my vapours with his hands gripping my shoulders. I announce an open invitation to all:

'Hey everybody! *Hic*-I'm sorry. Heycomeonlet'sgetalittlefuckedup-wooooo!'

October 2: Barcelona, Day Off

I awoke around noon.

What — in all seven levels of fuck have I done to myself?

My head hammered with the pangs of an anvil. My stomach roiled and protested. A while later I barfed into the toilet. My teeth felt furry.

At 7 p.m., I rose once more to praise the white bowl.

Dry heaves.

It's not what you think.

Okay, it's mostly what you think, but this isn't just a hangover. In truth, a gastrointestinal bug was circulating in Camp Cohen. I got it.

I had to piece together my night. It started at 7 p.m., and the only other record is an email. At 1.14 a.m., everything ended with the following message to Elaine:

"OMG SO FUCKED OMG. ME AND DUPUIS, OMG, THE UNRAVELLING OF THE WORLD, OMG... "

Usually when you feel this bad it's because you stayed up to 5 a.m.

I must be aging.

I didn't want to put anything in my belly, but the hunger was strong. There is no way I'm leaving this room. Room service.

A young lady brought me a tray of *penne all'arrabbiata* and a bottle of sparkling water.

I hoped she wasn't grossed out.

You know when you get used to your own filth? I didn't know if the room smelt like feet, or vomit, or what. My appearance was wretched enough: mismatched jim-jams, greying stubble and I've-just-been-arrested-hair. Death's assistant.

It took an hour to finish the bowl of pasta.

Usually I'd be like Hungry Hippos.

Self-induced torture exacerbated by stomach bug.

This, for a whole day

Life is fragile when it wants to be. The body can stand a bit of abuse but when it says no, it means it. It's like a rechargeable battery: the longer you leave the light on, the more frequently you need to recharge. There are only so many cycles of this process your body can endure before the lights go out for good.

Dan called me.

'How you doing?'

'Oh wonderful, like a turd in the dunes.'

Apparently the bug is a brief affair. It kisses the barf button, moves to the gut and eventually flushes itself out, leaving the host with a feeling of nausea.

I'm reflective in this brittle state.

It's folly to abuse yourself then regret it at the crossroads. How foolish to poison your body and soul then expect all to be well. How utterly mad, calling upon the gods to save you when the answer is to avoid devils.

How rash, the act of self-abuse and self-medication.

I declare: henceforth I shan't drink for like maybe a couple of days.

October 3: Barcelona, Show Day

Morning light streams through a one-inch crack in the blackout blind. I don't feel too awful. Maybe around 85%. Better than yesterday's zero.

Mano.

Vano.

Our hill-twisty climb to the venue gives us big vistas of Barcelona: an eternity of grey and tan buildings in a blue sphere.

We arrive at Palau Sant Jordi. The trucks have already pulled away from the *hole*. That's the articulate epithet assigned to a loading dock. No truck in the hole means they're all empty.

The stage was ready for the Winning Team. Carpets, risers, the rest.

Mano.

Forklifto.

The venue is spacious with an oval, dome-like roof cut with round windows. Our lighting trusses and speakers hang from gridwork, itself suspended by an impassable web of steel rope and structural pipe.

In each corner hangs a turbine-like thing. They look like Star Wars pod-racing vehicles. Or binoculars.

The stage sits at one end of the oval. The seats are a wash of grey barely contrasting with the concrete structure they sit on. Black stackable chairs make up the floor seating. After the gig they'll be swept away to make room for a sweaty sport of some kind.

Slap-back is everywhere and wherever it is, it's different from everywhere else. Each band member will have a different experience of the bowl's acoustic reflections.

The sweaty humidity is perfect for biting insects. As I chowed on lunch, bugs ate my ankles.

Paris seems like a long time ago, but we're only one gig past it. It's difficult to shake off the fetters of my Parisian guitar boo-boo. To be fair it wasn't the end of the world but as a backline tech you don't want to be responsible for things going bump. At the party the other night a few of us laughed at the various goofs we make from time to time. Leonard's encouraging conclusion: 'It happens to the best of us.'

SHOWTIME

It's hot. There's an oven in my hat. My face feels like it's been wiped down with olive oil and sprinkled with pepper. My trousers smell of bug repellant. I begin fantasising about the shower in my hotel bathroom: there's a marble slab to sit on. There you can hang your head and think about what you've done.

In Spain nothing ever happens on time.

It's already a pain in the ass going on at 9 p.m., and 9.15 is twisting the bayonet. When we finally get going the 12,000-strong crowd cheer and hoot during songs, after songs, and so much by the end of the first set they didn't hear Leonard clearly say he'd return for a second set. Much like Toulon, they think it's all over.

The obvious choice to lift them from confusion is Javier. Armed with a big smile he reappears on stage to make the announcement in Spanish.

The second set sees an interesting deviation. Charley sings some lead lines of *The Gypsy's Wife* normally handled by Leonard. The Webbs receive extended applause for their delivery of *Coming Back to You.*

People clap hands above their heads. During the encores they're on foot, drowning out the P.A. with their cheers.

Two shows remain and we're looking beyond Europe, to this place they call America, a little country sandwiched between Mexico and Canada; half grilled-cheese, half torta.

Conversations touch on new flightcases, sleeker truck-packs and fewer needless things.

All said we still have two shows this side of the Atlantic.

October 4: Travel to Madrid

My morning was quite different from many of late. This book started from blogs and most mornings were reserved for writing. Today I sat for a minute and took it in, not necessarily for a reader but for me. I sipped tea at the marina opposite the hotel. Sunrays weaved through an armada of gently swaying masts. I felt a quiet calm. The end was coming and I was glad of it.

What better way to augment the perfect morning than with the arbitrary rules of commercial flying.

I sat fastened to my seat, reading an ebook.

I know she's looking at me. An austere matron in her dark blue uniform appears in my periphery. Her grey hair looks like bat wings.

'Sir?'

I sigh in exasperation. 'Yes?'

'Please put that away.' She walked on, assuming I'd obey.

'How about I wait until you get the call.'

She turned. Her neck folded. 'I beg your pardon?'

I cracked my knuckles and simpered. 'Flight attendants take your seats.'

She tore back with puckered lips. 'What?'

'You guys do this all the time. You tell us to put away our devices — the only things keeping us sane in your flap-handed system of cattle-herding — and then we sit on the tarmac for half an hour waiting to take off. You get the run of the cabin while we sit with our knees pressed against the seat in front of us.'

She sighed. 'Sir we are very busy please put—'

'When the captain says *Flight attendants take your seats*, that's the real take-off cue. Until then I'm reading. Don't tell me a seven-seven-seven is going to buckle like a toddler learning to walk because of a Kindle. It's like an *Etch A Sketch* for fuck's sake.'

She glared. Her lips writhed like snakes.

I think she likes me. I wiggle my eyebrows and blow her a kiss.

The taser felt like a hundred scorpions.

I woke up with drool on my Kindle. Madrid was sunny and warm.

October 5: Madrid, Show Day

Wake up, shower, eat, tap the keys.

Van: clapped-out diesel piece of shit festooned with ancient band stickers; indecipherable logos.

Man: drives like a teenager on meth. He kicks the accelerator and stands on the brakes. He is surprised by red lights. The windscreen is filthy.

There's lots to see in Madrid if you aren't hurtling through streets at light speed. It's a parade of statues, arcs, and winged sentinels of stone.

Tyres scream against hot tarmac. Pedestrian crossing.

A skinny young man appears, eyes hidden behind black lenses. He wears red denim trousers, painted on.

He runs, literally runs, into the middle of the road, and we skid to a halt.

He's wearing a white sleeveless shirt. His hair is perfect. He stops — in the middle of the fucking crossing — to light a cigarette.

Spain.

Palacio de los Sports: terrible acoustics. You can buy oxygen in the cheap seats.

Around 8.30 p.m., Jon comes on the radio. There are people sitting in seats which were supposedly blocked out. It's a problem. Jon makes sure every seat in the house gets a good sound. In the mornings, the promoter hands out a seating map, showing Jon which seats are sold, and which will be blocked. He points P.A. speakers and fine-tunes accordingly.

Jon's peeved and rightly so. If the promoters ~~lie~~ neglect to inform us of seating changes, we look (or rather sound) bad.

Spain.

The show is delayed to 9.15. Eyes roll.

Spain.

SHOWTIME

During the second set there was a moment of confusion in the stage left wing. Leonard called *Guests,* but I didn't have its guitar ready for Mitch. A short silence and some faffery resulted. High drama.

The show finished a little after 1 a.m.

The Winning Team packed up and threw some crud into a truck.

Different man.

Different van.

Alarm set for 9 a.m.

One more show.

October 6: Travel to Lisbon

After a sluggish four hours of sleep it was time to rise. Hotel beds are nice compared to bus bunks, but the downside is commercial flying. Lisbon today.

Nothing happened on the way there.

We landed and went to the hotel.

Everyone did whatever everyone does, until they do something else.

I like to avoid group dining and this means eating early. Spain, Italy, Portugal — they eat late and it drives me nuts. Restaurants don't open until 7 or 8. I'm happy with a supermarket and shitty tofu dogs, anything but traipsing the streets in a group reluctant to commit.

This is the third time I've stayed in this hotel and I'm still unfamiliar with the area. If it isn't a glass-fronted seafood restaurant, it looks like a run-down brothel. If you knew how to look you might find a great restaurant hidden behind the façade of a condemned shoe shop. I won't because I don't care about finding culture two months into a tour. I want to go home where everything is familiar, tame, dull, dreary, wet, cloudy, and perhaps a little bit violent. I'm a dumb capitalist; give me logos and brands.

I set out from my room steeled for disappointment. At best I'll find a crone in a shop selling scurvy biscuits.

I ran into Joey in the lobby. He informed me there's a Hard Rock nearby — likely open. This is the best news I've had in ages.

I strolled along a triplet of parallel streets separated by pedestrian-friendly belts of palms, shrubs, grass, and little fountains. Under the foliage you can find a table and enjoy a light bite or drink. The stones under foot are organised in decorative patterns, a bit like *fleurs-des-lys*.

Portuguese looks a lot like Spanish, but doesn't much sound like it. You hear inflections of French, Spanish, and Russian. I guess it's something to do with Portugal's legacy of exploration.

Hard Rock.

I hear the angel choir.

I'm met by a lithe young woman with braced teeth and a flame tattoo on her right leg.

'Hey, welcome to Hard Rock, how you doing?' She's Portuguese but her inflections are affectations.

'Not so bad Flame-leg momma, how about you?'

'I'm seventeen.'

'Wasn't expecting that.'

She showed me to a table.

Tattooed lady-legs are in. Another waitress sports an eye-catching ink of two birds, one above each ankle. Fighting for space with her skirt's hem is a band of script around her thigh. I would try to decipher it but I'm at the age where creepy has legal implications.

Flame-leg takes my order of veggie burger, onion rings, and a smoothie.

She delivers the mint, strawberry and whatever-fruit-else drink, telling me she made it herself. Bless.

A perfect synchronicity. On the TV screens and blaring from speakers, Rod Stewart appears. He leads a gang of dirty ruffians overloading a motor vehicle. They stop in the middle of nowhere, moved to song by the appearance of legs. Hot legs.

The food filled a hole and off I went.

Nearby stands Teatro Eden, now apparently a hotel. Pink marble encloses tall palm trees. The frontage reminds me a little of the Hoover Building in West London, an art-deco affair.

On my stroll back to the hotel, a young man of good health and short hair stops me, offering to sell me a bullet of hash. The browny-green missile, the size of my thumb, is flawless like its salesman's skin.

I politely decline his offer.

'It's good stuff.'

'I don't smoke it.'

'It's a good price.'

'Yeah but I still don't smoke it.'

He looked over his shoulder and moved on.

I returned to the hotel and flopped about.

Last show tomorrow.

October 7: Lisbon Show

Man and van took us to the Pavilhao Atlantico.

Before we begin we're already talking about the final load-out.

Five truckloads of gear will need to be split up and scattered in different directions because not all of it is UHTC property. Lights and P.A. are hired, risers are hired, the trucks are hired. All of *our* stuff — backline, production, wardrobe, monitors, recording rigs — needs to go into two sea containers and sail to 'Merica.

Sea container dimensions are different to truck trailers, so it'll take a bit of thinking to pack the gear efficiently.

Fuck it, we'll be drunk.

Load-in this morning was scheduled for 7 o'clock but this is Portugal.

90 minutes later the riggers showed up. I guess they didn't get the message. Without riggers we can't hang P.A. or lights. And we can't really do anything until those are sorted. The riggers got into gear and things happened.

Until they didn't happen.

The stage right speaker array isn't high enough.

There are these things called electric chain-hoists, or *motors*. We (the *Royal We*) hang them in the roof. They lift speakers, lights, cable bridges, almost anything you want in the air. A *dead-hang* is ideal when fitting motors because it's quick and easy. When you can't get a dead-hang you employ a *bridle* which involves some trigonometry of weight distribution.

The bridle for the stage right speakers wasn't high enough and now the array has to be taken down so the bridle can be remade.

Leonard was supposed to soundcheck at 4 p.m. It's 5.45 instead.

Another hot, continuously sweaty, bowl of a room. The roofspace is like a ship's hull and echoes swirl within.

Soundcheck is finished around 7 p.m., bullshit.

If the riggers had shown up when they were supposed to...

I guess it was another ~~lie~~ miscommunication.

Portugal.

WHEN CAN WE GO HOME?

The final show of any tour feels like a gig too far. It's tempting to treat tonight like the last day of school but we can't — when you drop your guard you make misktaes. You have to fight off the selfish desire to hurry things along. You have to remind yourself all things will come about in due time. We have to treat tonight's show like any other. Mickey confirms this after visiting the boss in his dressing room. 'Be ready for anything.'

SHOWTIME

Delay.

Portugal.

I fear Leonard is going to throw the set into chaos. My mind whirls at the permutations of disorder he'll command on a whim. Is the baritone in Drop-C? Where's the capo? Damnit, is that spare tuned?

First set over. Nothing truly surprising.

Before the second set Mitch informs me *Guests* might make an appearance, so I prepare with the appropriate guitar.

Leonard skips *Heart With No Companion.* Mike plays harmonica on that number, and he doesn't know if the song is gone from the set entirely or if it will return. No one knows, probably not even Leonard.

GUITAR LOGISTICS

Every night I have to be aware of the set list and plan ahead. Usually after *Heart With No Companion* I'll take Mitch's Telecaster and drop-D it for *Democracy*. Both songs involve the guitar. But *Heart* didn't happen.

If *Heart* comes back, the guitar needs to be in standard tuning. If it's *Democracy*, drop-D.

What to do?

Roll the dice, leave it in standard tuning.

Of course the opposite of what I think happens.

'Democracy!' says the boss.

I take the guitar out to Mitch.

He grabs it. 'So it's not in drop-D?'

I reply with a nervous look. 'Yeah sorry I don't know what's going on.'

Time is ticking. Air is dead.

With a straight face and spring-loaded arm he ejects a cup of hot coffee on me

'Gah!' I scream. I reel back and protect my scalded face too late. He pegs my head with the empty mug. *Pank!*

Oof! Something hits me in the ass real hard. I turn to see Leonard, fresh from sticking the boot in.

'Take that, commie!'

I'm horrified. The guy is in his 70s, what am I supposed to do? 'Ow, dude!'

He's twirling the mic like a motorcycle chain. 'Get off my stage.'

The whole world is in on it. People are laughing and throwing vegetables, braying like farm animals, taking pleasure in watching the bully pig slaughtered.

'Is this it?' I cry among the chaos of injustice. 'Is this how it ends?'

Leonard cocks a half-grin. 'It's what you make it bro.'

Mitch whistles *It's a Long Way to Tipperary* and retunes the Telecaster himself. He turns to me; 'I told you I'd get you.'

The rest of the band are watching with folded arms.

They're blaming this all on me.

A roadie is supposed to win. Supposed to win. The cosmos is upturned.

I have no course but to limp away. The coffee burnt my balls. I'm dripping, half-blind, and I can already feel a crescent lump rising on my forehead.

I trip over a light and fall into the veil of sheer deceit, entangled in its web, flailing. 'Whyyyyy!?'

Javier joins in. Cackling, he throws a bottle of water.

Paf! in the face. The bottle explodes, water cascades, and I am electrically linked to the light.

It feels like a thousand scorpions.

Democracy begins with snare rolls.

This is the end.

It's shit.

My tombstone reads: *Be ready for anything*

October 8: Going Home

I guess I'm not dead.

I wolfed some brekkie.

Final man, final van.

At exactly 9 a.m., seven of us departed for the airport.

Back in August I was glad to get away from home. I'd spent much of the year as a househusband. This morning I look forward to washing dishes, eating simply, controlling my own laundry, yelling at the kids, yelling at the TV, and driving my '99 Polo on narrow, hedge-flanked roads.

Before all that I gotta leave Portugal.

Lisbon's Portela airport has a big footprint but low ceilings crammed with a mesh of aluminium tubing offer a dated, stuffy environment. It's another shopping mall with a couple of runways.

I'm in a queue for something. Behind me, a North American couple; she's maybe 45, he 50.

She wears a scowl like a bad tattoo.

His shoulders are slumped.

She carries two bags of fresh shopping.

He's carrying one — and everything else.

She exhales sharply, like this is all a conspiracy to get her. 'We should've put these in the big bags.'

He sighs, at length. He's so over this. 'When we get to the other side.'

She mumbles something, a retort.

He glowers. 'You're getting annoying.'

She spins and hisses in a hush. 'Oh — *I'm* getting annoying.'

I love this team. A packhorse with an opinion driven by an owner with no clue. They reinforce my travel beliefs. Pack light and don't buy shit for people.

Another queue.

We have to get one of those stupid buses to the plane. I'm watching the clock, aware I'm in Portugal. I'm pretty sure BA501 ain't leaving at 11 a.m. I'm convinced, I *know* it's delayed, but there's no official mention. I fear I'm going to miss my connection to Belfast.

In Japan and Germany you'd be flogged for allowing such a bumbling misuse of public time. In the UK and Ireland you expect a 50/50 split: either a loose form of punctuality or a hollow apology. In Italy, Spain, and Portugal you just expect a delay. Somewhere in the airport there's a guy smoking a cigarette who's not where he's supposed to be. But it's okay because it always happens. The sun-scorched hills are alive with not giving a shit.

Finally we get on the bendy cattle-bus and board a British Airways plane. The incessant and insincere apologies are an easing familiarity. Assuming I'll miss my flight to Belfast, I look for the silver lining. Fuck it, just get me north of Senlac Hill, Heathrow will do for now. As long as there's a pair of overpainted lips, thinly upturned in contempt behind a cash register in WH Smith I'll feel like I'm home.

I guess we made up the time. I didn't miss my flight. Nor was I surprised by my WH Smith experience. I approached the cash desk with a pack of Worcester sauce crisps. The male clerk clicked on a mouse and stared at a screen. Opening my velcro wallet was like clearing my throat.

He didn't flinch.

Neither did his counterpart dealing with a supply guy. They were immersed in separate worlds.

What cunts.

Were they on strike?

Who knows. I replaced the crisps and left completely baffled. If you're a manager there, it was at Terminal 1 near gate 8, around 2.45 p.m.

George Best Belfast City Airport.

Taxi. 5.45 p.m.

M2 motorway. Cave Hill to my left. Two months ago the sun would've been higher in the sky than it is now.

A8; the sun cools through the spectrum behind rolling hills.

Larne. My house appears.

I reconcile with a few heavy truths. It's been 63 days. There's no candy rainbow; no golden mane flowing in the breeze; certainly not enough world peace.

The shire proverb had yet to deliver; I've still to meet a man named Hammer with a persistent demand that I ask him the time; I was hit neither by bus, plane nor train.

There were no honeybees in sight.

Two months away from home and the only real difference is a dead washing machine. There had to be catch.

Cup of tea. I'm home.

Before I could truly relax I had a thought to purge: *WH Smith cunts.*

It's over.

What was this book?

There was a great deal of malarkey in this book. Some of what you read didn't happen, and some did. The only real jerk in here is me. Everyone else is cool. Call it dramatic licence.

There's a problem with writing a book like this. When I signed a contract in 2008, there was a confidentiality clause. You can't dish the dirt, but you want to talk about something. In the first edition of *No Ideas*, and indeed the blogs that began it all, I tried to be everybody's friend. I felt I had to paint a fun and congenial picture of life on the road. Worse, I wanted to appear deep, like a cornucopia of perspicacity, like I *belonged* on a Leonard Cohen tour. The last thing I wanted to do was bring Leonard into disrepute.

But something dawned on me: just how, in the nine levels of jack-fuckery, is a guy like me going to do that? Who the hell is going to say they liked Leonard Cohen until they read my book? What was I thinking? The character narrating the original book was someone I grew to dislike. He wasn't a roadie, he was trying his damnedest to be anything but.

People who've read the blogs from the start; maybe they'll hate this book. Maybe I'm fine with that. It's just a book. It's not aimed at anyone; it's crass and offensive, like a genuinely road-weary backline tech.

I'm still glad to have been nurtured by the road. It's filled with funny, endlessly talented, and downright crazy people. Artists don't live their lives according to arbitrary standards, they pursue expression and individuality. We backline roadies eat, work and drink with those people and they rub off on us. We're also practical and technically minded, so we're like half-breeds. Backline people don't really *belong* anywhere.

Not only am I thankful to the road in general, there are people who deserve special mention.

I owe a portion of my world to Leonard Cohen himself. Without him I wouldn't be who I am now. Without his easy-going touring schedule I'd never have taken up online university courses and picked up the confidence to really write for an audience. Without him I wouldn't have the *chutzpah* to write this stupid book.

I must re-thank the people who encouraged me to keep writing in the first place. They're all mentioned in the first version of the book so I shan't repeat their names here. They might hate this version.

Special and ongoing thanks of course go to Elaine, Lars, and Vala.

My mum for pointing out some humdinger typos.

My late stepdad Davy, without whom I'd never have landed in Northern Ireland.

My dad, for introducing me to the concept of enunciation and for pointing out that I have a proclivity for superfluous commas.

Sharon Erde for telling me to work harder.

Lastly I must thank you for making it this far.

That's it.

#0056 - 300818 - C0 - 210/148/7 - PB - DID2290628